Dr Hansdev Patel

# GOLFING
## IN
# MOROCCO

Land of peaceful and rewarding golfing holidays

Photography : Aziz Boumousse

Watercolours by Bryan Thatcher

THE AUTHOR - DR HANSDEV PATEL

THE ARTIST - BRYAN THATCHER

THE PHOTOGRAPHER - AZIZ BOUMOUSSE

THE DESIGNER - JODI PHILLIPS

# GOLFING
## IN
# MOROCCO

BY DR HANSDEV PATEL

ALL YOU NEED TO KNOW:

**HOW TO GET THERE.**

**COURSE INFORMATION**

**RECOMMENDED TRAVEL COMPANIES**

**RECOMMENDED HOTELS**

**RECOMMENDED RESTAURANTS**

**PLACES OF INTEREST**

Windsor & Peacock Publishers

London

Design: Jodi Phillips

Printed and Bound in England by: Butler & Tanner Ltd

ISBN Number: 0-9537985-2-6

Windsor & Peacock Ltd

Art & Travel Publishers

14 South Approach

Moor Park Northwood

Middlesex HA6 2ET

England

Telephone: +44 (0) 1923 836064

Fax: +44 (0) 1923 836063

www.windsor-peacock.com

# GOLFING
## IN
# MOROCCO

Dr Hansdev Patel

Photography: Aziz Boumousse

Watercolours by Bryan Thatcher

## CONTENTS

# ACKNOWLEDGEMENTS

Many people have enthusiastically contributed significantly to the production of a book of this magnitude and complexity, not least the officials of the golf clubs, hotels travel companies and restaurants represented in the book. Too numerous to mention by name, I am nonetheless, deeply grateful to them for their collective goodwill and co-operation. A sentiment echoed by the Publishers, Windsor & Peacock Ltd.

No Golf course or establishment is fixed in time and although I have tried to keep abreast of changes, I offer my apologies if any of the details in the book are inaccurate.

First and foremost, a special thanks to my wife, Paru, for her unrelenting patience, encouragement and support extending from pacing the golf courses to sub-editing to photo selection and finally book critic!

Warm thanks are due to Mrs Fathia Bennis at the Morocco National Tourist Office in Rabat for her calm, gentle and encouraging support and to Mr Mostafa Raguigue for his professionalism, efficiency and helpfulness, without whom this project would not have been possible. He opened many doors for me in England and Morocco. He has become a dear friend. I found that both Mostafa and Fathia have a genuine deep-seated love for Morocco and a passion to share with the rest of us, all that their wonderful country and the friendly people have to offer to their visitors.

Mr El Kasmi, Director of the Tourist Office in London for his unconditional help and support and to all his staff especially Mr Aziz Mnii.

I am indebted to Royal Air Maroc for their services. The Chairman, Mr Mohamed Berrada in Casablanca and Abdelhamid Khalil General Manager at their London office, deserve a special mention and I am most appreciative of their help and generous support. Thanks also to Maryse Bergel for taking care of all my travel arrangements.

Jean Faivre and all the staff at the Hilton Hotel in Rabat not only for their flawless hospitality and impeccable service during my stay with them but also for their support in the publication of this book.

I am most grateful to Brigitte Raguigue for compiling a list of recommended hotels, restaurants and car hire companies in Morocco and for proof reading.

Mukesh Patel, Gary Edelman, Robert Saldanha and Alan Hart of Sandy Lodge Golf Club for their frank and honest opinions and generally for their excellent company and friendship on and off the golf course.

Thanks to Mr Mohammed Phaytan and Mr Mohammed Fakir for their generous help and support and to Alecoss Travel of London who are destined to become synonymous with Golfing Holidays to Morocco.

The management and staff of all the Golf Courses mentioned in the book for allowing me free and easy access to all their facilities. A special thank you to Mr Bouftas and Mr Addi Jabor of the Royal Dar Es Salam in Rabat.

Thank you to the staff and proprietors of Tikida Beach Hotel in Agadir, Hotel El Minzah in Tangier, Hotel Transatlantic in Meknes, Hotel Sol Melia Karam in Ouarzazate, Hotel Sofital in El Jadida and Palmeraie Golf Palace Hotel in Marrakech for looking after me and for their generous hospitality during my visits.

Ahmed Bikane and Said Oubacher of B.B.Tours for their safe and professional chauffeuring services.

Aziz Boumousse has produced some wonderful photographs for the book. Through his work here this unassuming and very creative individual deserves to make a name for himself in the photographic world.

Thanks to Kate Lewis for sub-editing and secretarial help and to Mish Yanni for his design input.

Jodi Phillips is an accomplished contemporary artist and designer. She has brought in a fresh young image to this book. Together with the traditional very "English" watercolours by the famous watercolour artist, Bryan Thatcher; I hope the look and feel of the book will have a wide appeal and encourage the reader to visit Morocco and to experience all it has to offer.

Hansdev Patel

May 2002

# HIS MAJESTY MOHAMMED VI
# KING OF MOROCCO

Sidi Mohammed, eldest son of Morocco's King Hassan II, was born in Rabat on August 21, 1963.

In 1985, he obtained a B.A in law at the Rabat Mohammed V University; his research project being entitled "the Arab-African Union and the Strategy of the Kingdom of Morocco in matters of International Relations."

In 1987, he obtained a higher degree in Political Sciences. In 1993, he was awarded the title of Doctor in law at the French University of Nice-Sophia Antipolis for his thesis on "EEC-Maghreb Relations."

He began representing his father, the late King Hassan II (who ruled from 1961 to 1999), in 1974 at different international occasions.

Crown Prince Sidi Mohammed ascended the throne on the day of his father's death (July 23rd 1999), under the name of Mohammed VI, becoming the 18th king of the Sharifian dynasty since 1664.

Following in their father's footsteps both HM Mohammed VI and his brother HH Prince Moulay Rachid are keen golfers and are often seen playing on their "home" course - The Royal Dar Es Salam in Rabat.

# WELCOME

Mrs Fathia Bennis – Directeur General

Morocco National Tourist Board

Rabat

Morocco

It is a real pleasure for me to introduce you to Morocco, a land of wonders, through this book, dedicated to our country's golfing legacy. This new book will undoubtedly help to convey the famous glamour and romance of our Kingdom.

Morocco and the United Kingdom have had a long-standing friendly relationship. Many British artists, politicians and businessmen have made Morocco their second home, having fallen under its spell! The most famous is certainly Mr Winston Churchill whose name is clearly now associated with the Mamounia Palace Hotel in Marrakesh. However, Morocco also attracts creative people, like the famous Scottish Artist, James McBey and the Irish born Sir John Lavery RA, for "inspiration", "light", culture, colours, fragrances, easy going relaxed lifestyle etc.

In fact, our historical links with the United Kingdom date from the 17th century, when England inherited the city of Tangiers from the Portuguese, as part of Catherine of Braganza's dowry on her marriage to Charles II. Even after withdrawing from the City 20 years later, the British always remained on friendly terms with Morocco and did all they could to uphold the authority of the Sultan of Tangier and stop any other European power from colonising it.

Evidence of this relationship still exists in Tangiers where, at the beginning of the 20th century, the Golf course was built and created by the British in 1917.

Since then, Morocco has continued to develop its golfing assets, to become one of the leading international golf destinations. It seems apt that we refer to the British when it comes to presenting our country's varied golf landscapes, due to the British tradition of being great travellers and the first golfers in the world!

I trust that this book will captivate your imagination and convince you to come to Morocco and experience its magic for yourself. You will be our treasured guest and always and everywhere welcomed.

# WELCOME

I am delighted to have the opportunity to introduce you to "GOLFING IN MOROCCO", a valuable reference book to Golf in a country where hospitality is a main feature. Through its words and pictures you will have the pleasure of appreciating the richness of Morocco and its greens.

Morocco and golf go hand in hand: whilst playing golf on outstanding courses scattered all over Morocco you are also able to discover a magnificent country with a rich cultural background, coupled with a pleasant climate particularly favourable for golfing throughout the year.

Fully dedicated to serving and promoting Morocco and convinced that golfing is to be one of the most important tourist attractions of Morocco we, Royal Air Maroc, are your Gateway to your leisure sport in our country.

With our growing Network of world-wide destinations, our comprehensive internal flights and a modern fleet we bring the experience of golfing in Morocco within your reach.

Let me now wish you an enjoyable read till we can welcome you on board.

**Mr Mohamed Berrada**
Chairman Chief Executive
Royal Air Maroc
Casablanca
Morocco

# WELCOME

El Mostafa Raguigue
Morocco National Tourist Board
Rabat
Morocco

MOROCCO: Land of peaceful and rewarding Golf holidays

In todays busy world, people more than ever look to recreational and leisure opportunities for an escape from their bustling environment and everyday concerns. People have become more discerning about their holiday requirements and it is becoming harder to find one single country, which can meet visitors' wide ranges of expectations and needs.

Everyone seeks a year-round benign climate and a safe and peaceful environment. We could say that Morocco has it all: a friendly welcome, short travelling times, excellent facilities, a relaxed atmosphere, all with the impact of a tremendous variety of scenery and cultural influences.

When it comes to Golf both as a leisure pastime and the main holiday activity, we have chosen to make this sport highly significant in our country and to promote "Golf" as one of our natural assets.

Strategically located in the western part of North Africa, Morocco is the "African" country closest to the Old World, being only a few miles across the Straights of Gibraltar. Thanks to its magnificent and diverse scenery, ranging from high mountains to arid deserts, with many miles of sandy coasts and extensive plains, our country exhibits all types of climates and influences. Morocco displays fascinating physical and cultural evidence of its thousands of years of civilisation, in the form of historical sites, architecture, gastronomy, folklore and the arts.

Tourism being one of the country's main priorities, the Moroccan National Tourist Board has particularly focused its attention on the fastest growing sector of this industry, namely golf.

Golf is a long-lasting tradition in our country, with courses dating back from the 20's, for example, Tangiers and a lot of "Royal" ones. The late King Hassan II was the first golfer of the Kingdom of Morocco. He inaugurated, in the early 70s, the prestigious Trophy, which is named after him and this event has celebrated its 30th anniversary in 2001. The Trophy has elevated Morocco to an internationally recognised golf destination of quality.

A lot of our public and private operators now understand the added value that golfing can bring and investment in equipment etc. is constantly being developed.

Today Morocco's rich and varied golf courses cover all the regions of the country and tourists will have to visit the country several times to experience the various pleasures of them all…

To summarise the substantial resources of Morocco as a privileged golf destination for visitors worldwide and which has already been awarded, by the Industry professionals in 1998 with the title the "best emerging Golf destination", we emphasise the courses themselves. These are diverse and of quality; they are well-maintained; the friendly staff will go out of their way to extend hospitality to guests; the booking availability and catering facilities are good; and, of course, the climate is always sunny and clement; Morocco's fascinating mixture of history, culture and art enhances a holiday destination which has political stability, personal safety and a tourism industry that is developing all the time.

Fully committed to promote Morocco as an expanding golf destination, the Moroccan National Tourist Office strategy is the perfect expression of Government initiatives to strengthen Tourism.

We are confident in our country's future in this area and hope this book will persuade its readers to come and experience some peaceful, rewarding and pleasurable Moroccan golf holidays.

## GOLFING IN MOROCCO

# INTRODUCTION

Golf was first introduced into Morocco at the beginning of the century - even before football- and has since become a national passion. It was the favourite sport of His Majesty King Hassan II, who acquired international ranking by creating the competition held in November at the Royal Dar es-Salam in Rabat for the elegant and much prized Hassan II trophy - a jewel-encrusted, golden dagger. The Moroccan Open is held in January and is now a permanent fixture on the PGA European Tour.

The enthusiasm of the King and the Royal Family for golf, led to many courses sprouting near major cities and resorts throughout the country, including one in the Palace Grounds! When a ruling Monarch has a passion for the sport, only the best will do. So, using the best golf course designers and architects in the world, masters such as Robert Trent Jones, Cabell B. Robinson and Jack Nicklaus, the most picturesque parts of the country were cordoned off and converted into magnificent golf courses. The Royal Dar es Salam is now ranked as one of the top 50 courses in the world.

Morocco is one of the best-kept secrets in the Golfing world. Less then 3 hours away from England, an exotic holiday destination par excellence with impeccably groomed and virtually uncrowded golf courses of distinction and immense variety - the snows of the Atlas forming the backdrop to the Marrakech Courses; fairways carved through a forest of Cork and Oak Trees in Rabat, on the golden dunes at Agadir and floodlit in the Palace Grounds of Meknes. This safe and peaceful country, possessing an ideal climate and people who are welcoming and friendly, is also known for great cuisine. It has a well established infra structure that would be the envy of many holiday golf destinations. A fascinating country to see and discover for both the golfer and the non-golfer, where the desert meets the sea and East meets West, just one hour from Gibraltar.

There are now 18 courses in the country with many more on the drawing board. A round usually costs Dr300-Dr400 plus around Dr100 for a caddy. It is obligatory to use a local caddy. Each course employs enough to cater for every player, even on the busiest days!

## MOROCCO - THE LAND,
## THE PEOPLE, THE HISTORY

The Kingdom of Morocco is located on the northwestern corner of Africa. Morocco's maximum length from northeast to southwest is 2500km, and its maximum width from east to west is 765 km. The country borders Algeria (east and south east) and Mauritania (south); its western border is defined by the Atlantic Ocean, and its northern border by the Mediterranean Sea. Morocco faces Spain across the Strait of Gibraltar to the north. The capital is Rabat. Population of Morocco is officially estimated at a little over 29 million.

Morocco is the ideal starting point for the traveller to Africa. An easy hop from Europe, it can be a friendly, hectic and stimulating place to get around in. Open-air markets throughout the country are piled high with rugs, woodwork, and jewellery, also making it a shopper's paradise.

## FACTS AT A GLANCE

Full country name: Kingdom of Morocco

Area: 710,000 sq km

Population: 29 million

Capital city: Rabat

People: 55% Arabian, 44% Berber, 0.8% foreigners, 0.2% Jews

Languages: Arabic (officially) with Berber dialects, as well as French, Spanish and English.

Religion: Islam

Government: Constitutional monarchy

Head of State: King Mohammed VI

# THE LAND

Morocco is spectacularly diverse.

Morocco's mountains are the highest in northern Africa and occupy more than one third of the nation's total land area. The famous Atlas Mountains synonymous with Morocco are in the centre of the country.

Morocco's lowlands and rocky plateaux are dominated by the Atlas Mountain system. Only in the fertile alluvial lowlands, which occupy about one fifth of the total land area, is intensive agricultural cultivation possible. The country's lowlands include those of the Moulouya (Northeast), Rharb (Northwest), the piedmont plains of the High Atlas (central), and the Sous plain (Southwest). Rocky plateaux (with average elevations approaching 3,000 feet [9,100 m]) cover almost half of the total land area and include the high plateau of eastern Morocco, the coastal plateau of Rabat, and the semi-arid Sahara plateau in the south.

All Moroccan rivers are torrential in nature, and they generally flow to the Atlantic Ocean or disappear in the Sahara—except for the Moulouya in the north, which flows into the Mediterranean Sea.

A Mediterranean climate with warm, wet winters and hot, dry summers prevails over most of northern and central Morocco, giving way to semiarid and desert climate in the south. The annual range of average monthly temperatures is 63° to 73° F (17° to 23° C) along the coasts and 50° to 80° F (10° to 27° C) in the interior. Annual precipitation ranges from 32 inches (800 mm) in the north to 8 inches (200 mm) in the south and half of this amount or less along the Sahara in the Southeast.

Forests cover about one fifth of the country's total area. Important species include cedar, fir, and juniper in the mountains and wild olive, cork oak, and dwarf palm at lower elevations. Wildlife includes mouflon (a wild sheep), gazelle, fennec (a type of fox), and macaco (a type of monkey) in the Atlas region.

## THE PEOPLE

The original people of Morocco are the Berbers, mainly nomadic tribes and famously fierce. From the 7th century AD, Arabs and Berbers have shared the country and alternately held power. Morocco's predominant ethno-linguistic group is made up of the offspring from centuries of inter-marriage between these two races and many people therefore speak both Arabic and Berber. Less-assimilated Berbers comprise about one third of the population. These people live in the mountains, where their Berber language has been preserved. They fall into three groups: the Rif people of the Rif Mountains, the Tamazight of the Middle Atlas, and the Shluh of the High Atlas and the Sous valley. The country's French and Spanish minorities have diminished significantly since Morocco's independence in 1956; other minorities include Bedouin Arabs and Africans. Most of the country's substantial Jewish minority emigrated to the state of Israel by the end of the 20th century. Arabic is the nation's official language. Most Moroccans are Sunnite Muslims of the Malikite order.

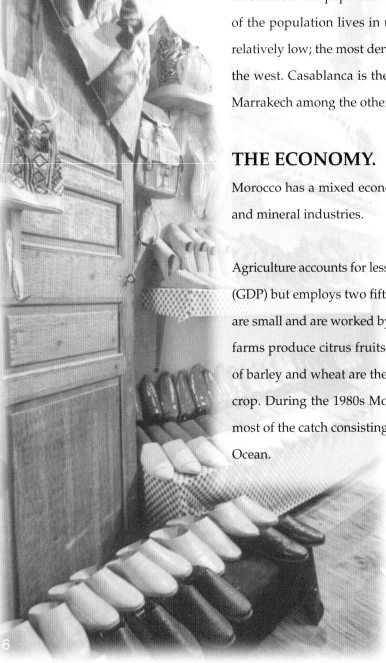

Two fifths of the population is younger than 15 years of age. Almost half of the population lives in urban areas. Overall population density is relatively low; the most densely settled areas being the urban centres of the west. Casablanca is the nation's largest city, with Rabat, Fès, and Marrakech among the other large urban centres.

## THE ECONOMY.

Morocco has a mixed economy largely based on services, agriculture, and mineral industries.

Agriculture accounts for less than one fifth of the gross domestic product (GDP) but employs two fifths of the workforce. Most farms in Morocco are small and are worked by families. Government-subsidised irrigated farms produce citrus fruits, wine, and vegetables for export. Harvests of barley and wheat are the chief staples and sugar beet is also a major crop. During the 1980s Morocco developed its fishing industry, with most of the catch consisting of sardines and mackerel from the Atlantic Ocean.

Morocco is the world's largest exporter of phosphate rock, or phosphorite, which is made into phosphate fertilisers for use in agriculture. Iron ore, lead, cobalt, zinc, manganese, and silver are also mined. Morocco's production of petroleum meets only a small fraction of its domestic demand.

Manufacturing industries account for approximately one fifth of the GDP and employ one sixth of the workforce. Industries are dominated by the production of phosphates. Casablanca is the nation's industrial and commercial centre, with light industries predominating there. The government has encouraged the development of industries outside Casablanca and has liberal codes regulating foreign investment. Small-scale industries employ most of the industrial workforce and produce light consumer goods. Chief manufactures include petroleum products, cement, textiles, processed foods, and chemicals. Electricity is generated primarily from imported fuels; little more than one tenth is generated from hydroelectric power.

Morocco's transportation network is highly developed, especially among the cities of the north and west. There is an excellent and a continually expanding motorway network. The principle ports include Agadir, Casablanca, and Tangier, all of which also have international airports. The government operates the very efficient railways.

## GOVERNMENT.

Morocco secured independence from France and Spain in 1956. In 1962, King Hassan put forward a new constitution, describing Morocco as a Muslim Sovereign State and a social democratic and constitutional monarchy. King Mohammed VI, son of the late King Hassan ll, now governs the Muslim Kingdom. Legislative power is vested in the House of Representatives, two-thirds of its members directly elected and one-third chosen by an Electoral College.

## HISTORY.

Unlike other North African countries, Morocco has been largely occupied by one people for as long as recorded history can recall. The Berbers settled the area thousands of years ago and at one time controlled all of the land between Morocco and Egypt. Divided into clans and tribes, they have always jealously guarded their independence. This fierce independence has helped preserve one of Africa's most fascinating cultures.

The early Berbers were unmoved by the colonising Phoenicians along the Mediterranean coast during the 12th century BC, and Carthage had settlements along the Atlantic coast in the 5th century BC. After the fall of Carthage, Morocco became a loyal ally of Rome under the Berber King Juba II (25 BC–Ad 24). In 46AD, Rome annexed Morocco as part of the province of Mauretania, and it is thought that the province was almost entirely Christianised during the latter part of Roman rule.

Islam burst onto the world stage in the 7th century, when the Arab armies swept out of Arabia, quickly conquering Egypt and reaching Morocco in the late 7th Century. The Arabs controlled all of North Africa by the start of the 8th century; however, by the next century much of North Africa had fragmented.

In 740 AD , the Berbers revolted against the rule of the Umayyads of Damascus and the Berbers remained independent of Umayyad and Abbasid rule. After some three centuries of local wars of conquest and shifting control, a Berber confederation known as the Almoravids conquered all of Morocco in the middle of the 11th century and enforced their rule over the Muslim areas of Spain as well.

In the early 12th century another Berber clan, the Almohads, revolted against the Almoravid dynasty, becoming the rulers of Morocco and all Muslim Spain. They were gradually driven from Spain in the 13th century and were defeated in Morocco in 1269 by the Marinids. Under the Marinids' rule, which lasted to the mid-15th century, Muslim mysticism, or Sufism, developed in Morocco. After the fall of the Marinids, the country was divided into small independent states until the Sa'dis established their rule over Morocco for a century after about 1550.

European intervention in North Africa increased in 1830. Great Britain obtained favourable trading rights from Morocco in 1856, and the Spanish increased their northern African territory at the expense of Morocco in 1859. In 1912 the sultan of Morocco, Moulay Abd al-Hafid, accepted French protectorate status.

Moroccan nationalism began to grow during and after World War II, and independence from France was negotiated in 1956, with Sultan

Sidi Muhammad V forming a constitutional government. In 1961 Moulay Hassan succeeded his father as Hassan II.

Hassan II was one of the great rulers of the last century and died on 23 July 1999, aged 70.

Mohammed VI ascended the Moroccan throne just before his 35th birthday.

Mohammed VI is the latest in a long dynastic line of Alawites. He plays a double role as temporal leader (King) and spiritual and moral guide, thanks to his family's direct lineage to Hussein ibn Ali, the grandson of the Prophet Mohammed. The religious significance of Mohammed VI's ancestry should not be underestimated and goes part of the way to explaining how his family has stayed in power so long and is much loved by the people of Morocco.

ROYAL GOLF CLUB MOHAMMEDIA

# IN AND AROUND CASABLANCA

## CASABLANCA

Thanks to Hollywood and the 1942 Humphrey Bogart, Ingrid Bergman film, Casablanca conjures up an image of smoke filled piano bars, easy living, romance, adventure all set in a steamy tropical climate. Nothing could be further from the reality.

Casablanca is a modern city, with a skyline dominated by towering office blocks and sprawling suburbs. Casablanca dominates the national economy, it is the chief port, and the financial, industrial, commercial and manufacturing centre of the Kingdom. International business deals are made here, luxury outlets are a plenty, leading edge industries are here, the biggest hotels, International conventions centres, Casablanca truly incarnates Modern Morocco.

Although a number of tourist establishments would lead you to believe otherwise, no scene of the film Casablanca was shot in Morocco, nor does the film bear any relation to the city of the past or the present. The film was released in 1942 at the time of the Casablanca landings and the Allied conference held here.

Most of Morocco's coastal towns and cities were occupied and even founded, by European powers and this is reflected in their appearance and feel. Long used to sight of foreigners, the people of Coastal Cities present a very different face to those of the interior. Rabat and Casablanca are both cosmopolitan centers at the heart of modern Morocco.

'Casa' shares the Mohammed V airport with Rabat, and regular flights are available to and from Europe and the Middle East. There are car hire agencies, cash machines and banks at the airport-but no hotel.

From the airport, take a grand taxi to the city center.

## MUST SEE IN CASABLANCA:

### THE HASSAN II GRAND MOSQUE

This massive edifice dominates Casablanca's skyline. No matter where you're staying, you're bound to see it from any upper floor thanks to its attention-grabbing green-tiled roof.

It is the third-largest mosque in the world. The mosque is well worth a visit and has the added attraction of being one of the very few religious buildings open to non-Muslims.

### OLD MEDINA.

The simple whitewashed houses of the medina, particularly those closest to the harbor, provide  an extraordinary contrast to Morocco's economic and commercial nerve center, just a few hundred yards away. The medina is small compared with other medinas in Morocco, but is definitely worth a visit.

### PLACE MOHAMMED V

Place Mohammed V was formerly called Place Nations Unis and vice versa, and the old names still appear on some maps. This is Casablanca's version of London's Trafalgar Square. There is an illuminated fountain, lots of pigeons, and a series of impressive buildings, with a blend of French colonial and traditional Moroccan styles inspired by art deco,(known as Mauresque architecture).

# RECOMMENDED

# PLACES TO STAY

**Royal Mansour Méridien – 5***
27 Avenue des F.A.R.
Tel (212) (22) 31 30 11
Fax (212) (22) 31 48 18

**Sheraton – 5***
100 Ave des F.A.R.
Tel (212) (22) 31 78 78 / (212)
(22) 31 51 37

**Hyatt Regency – 5***
Place des Nations Unies
Tel (212) (22) 26 12 34 / Fax
(212) (22) 20 44 46

**Riad Salam –4 ***
*(and Thalassotherapy Center*
*« Le Lido)*
Boulevard de la Corniche
Tel (212) (22) 39 13 13
Fax (212) (22) 39 13 45

## MOROCCAN CUISINE

Moroccan restaurants of the major hotels

**Al Mounia**
95 Rue du Prince Moulay
Abdellah
Tel (212) (22) 22 26 69

**Riad Zitoun**
31 Bd Rachidi
Tel (212) (22) 22 39 27

**Imilchil**
27 Rue Vizir Tazi
Tel (212) (22) 22 09 99

## SPANISH CUISINE

**La Java**
Bd Abdellatif Ben kaddour
Tel (212) (22) 94 27 11

**La Bodega**
133 Rue Allal Ben Abdellah
Tel (212) (22) 54 18 42

**La Corrida**
59 Rue El Arrar
Tel (212) (22) 27 81 55

## ITALIAN CUISINE

**Villa fandango**
Rue de La Mer Egée, La corniche
Tel (212)(22) 39 85 08

**Le Fellini**
36 Rue Moussa Ben Nousseir,
Gautier
Tel (212) (22) 25 31 28

**Toscana**
7 Rue Haala Elifrani, Racine
Tel (212) (22) 36 95 92

**I III Camelli's**
5 Rue Al Moutanabi, Gautier
Tel (212) (22) 49 15 65

**Il Piccolo Teatro**
Centre 2000
Tel (212) (22) 27 65 36

## FRENCH AND SEA FOOD CUISINE

**La Mer**
Bd de la corniche, Phare d'El
Hank
Tel (212) (22) 36 33 15

**Le Cabestan**
Bd de la Corniche, Phare d'El
Hank
Tel (212) (22) 39 11 90

**A ma Bretagne**
Bd de l'Océan Atlantique, Sidi
Abd-er-Rahmane
Tel (212) (22) 36 21 22

**La Réserve**
Bd de la Corniche, Aïn Diab
Tel (212) (22) 36 71 10

**La Brasserie Bavaroise**
133 Rue Allal Ben Abdellah
Tel (212) (22) 31 17 60

**Retro 1900**
Centre 2000
Tel (212) (22) 27 60 73

**Le Balcon 33**
Bd de la Corniche
Tel (212) (22) 36 72 05

**La Taverne du dauphin**
115 Bd Houphouët Boigny
Tel (212) (22) 22 12 00

**Le Port de Pêche**
(inside the Harbour)
Tel (212) (22) 31 85 61

**Ostréa**
(inside the Harbour)
Tel (212) (22) 44 13 90

# RECOMMENDED PLACES TO EAT

## ASIAN CUISINE

**Le Kim Mon**
160 Ave Mers Sultan
Tel (212) (22) 26 32 26

**Au Nid d'Hirondelle**
384 Bd Mohamed Zerktouni
Tel (212) (22) 20 64 42

**La Tonkinoise**
Ave de la Côte d'Emeraude, Aïn
Diab
Tel (212) (22) 39 11 87

**Le Bambou**
44 Bd d'Anfa
Tel (212) (22) 26 15 60

## BARS AND DISCOS

Night clubs of the Hotels

**Jazz Club Amstrong**
Rue Quiberon
Tel (212) (22) 39 76 56

**Le Casablanca**
Hôtel Hyatt Regency
Tel (212) (22) 26 12 35

**Le Vanity**
Bd de la Corniche

**La Notte**
Bd de la Corniche

**Villa Fandango**
Rue de la mer Egée, La corniche
Tel (212) (22) 39 85 08

# GOLF COURSES IN AND AROUND CASABLANCA

Royal golf of Anfa

Royal golf of Mohammedia: 25 km from Casablanca

Royal golf of Benslimane: located 30 km from Casablanca.

The Royal golf Universitaire of Settat: located 75 km from Casablanca.

The Golf Courses of Rabat and surrounds are also within easy reach.

Par 35

Meters: 2710

Green fees

Holes: 9

Caddy available

Closed Mondays

# THE ANFA ROYAL GOLF CLUB

Anfa-Casablanca Racecourse

Tel.: (212) 22 36 53 55 -  (212) 22 36 10 26

Fax: (212) 22 39 33 74

This little course, set inside a racetrack, is just a 10 minute drive from the centre of Casablanca. The course is located in one of Casablanca's finest residential districts which is famous for the 1947, Franklin Delano Roosevelt, Winston Churchill, Charles De Gaulle and Honore Giraud meeting in the nearby Anfa Hotel.

Perched on Anfa Hill, Royal Anfa has been played since 1937. This testing 9-hole course, 2710 metres par 35 course is very well maintained and not as easy to play as it first appears. From the putting green outside the clubhouse, one has to cross the track to reach the first tee, whereas the location of a few of the other tees requires a drive over the track!  The course demands accuracy and imagination to avoid the palm trees, eucalyptus and numerous flowering shrubs dotted around the course.

There are excellent facilities in the clubhouse, including tennis courts, swimming pool and an impressive view over the fairways and the lush gardens of the golf course.  The imposing minaret of the Hassan II Mosque forms a backdrop.

A haven of peace and tranquillity in the heart of a busy City, The Royal Anfa is a must for a golfer on a business trip. Golf Clubs are available for hire.

# ROYAL GOLF DE MOHAMMEDIA

BP12 Mohammedia

Tel.: (212) 23 32 4656

Fax:  (212) 23 32 1102

Beyond an imposing entrance lies ones of Morocco's finest golf courses - the 18 hole Royal Mohammedia Golf Course in the 'City of Flowers'. It is located, an easy taxi ride away, on the Atlantic coast, 20km North of Casablanca.

Named in the honour of the then ruling monarch, the course was established in 1924 as a 9-hole course and later extended to 18 holes. The person responsible for the present layout is a mystery, a pity because he deserves recognition for creating a masterpiece.

The Royal Mohammedia Golf Club is part of the Mohammedia –Anfa Royal Golf Club. It offers challenging golf for the experts and enjoyable golf for the leisure golfers. It is a parkland course with links features, undulating fairways, small greens and golfers must always make allowance for the constant year round Atlantic breeze. This is a course, which would make golfers from Scotland feel at home.

Par 72

Meters: 5917

Green fees

Holes: 18

Caddy available

Closed Tuesdays

Closed Mondays

Eucalyptus, pine and mimosa trees abound, as well as cactus-covered sand dunes, which form part of the rough. It is rare in the golf world to find such a varied environment.

All the holes are outstanding. The layout is always different and absorbing. With the wild sea as the backdrop, the greens are protected by a whole variety of brightly coloured flowering plants. The smell of pine trees makes playing this course a truly memorable experience.

The Royal Mohammedia golf Club is also the home to several national and international competitions.

English-speaking professionals are available. The gracious clubhouse has a welcoming veranda and its excellent restaurant and bar completes a most appealing picture of Moroccan golf at its finest.

## BEN SLIMANE ROYAL GOLF CLUB

Avenue des F.A.R.

BP 83

Ben Slimane

Tel.: (212) 23 32 8793

Fax: (212) 23 29 7225

It is well worth the one hour or so drive, equidistant from both Casablanca and Rabat, to play this wonderful course, which in a few years time will mature into being one of the premier courses of Morocco. The visitor is greeted by a breathtaking view across a green and beautiful valley. Flocks of ducks, who have made the Ben Slimane Royal Golf course their home, can be seen flying and taking off in the distance.

Water is the main feature of the Ben Slimane Royal Club. Robert von Hagge designed this newly established 18-hole course with plans for a further 9 holes. The clubhouse has to be one of the best in country, in prime location with stunning views across the course and the surrounding countryside, from its elevated position. Full catering facilities are offered and there is a genuinely pleasant and relaxed atmosphere.

Par 72

Meters: 6403

Green fees

Holes: 18

Caddy available

Closed Mondays

A huge lake stretches the length of the golf course along with a series of smaller ones, some manmade and others natural, which dominates many of the holes. It is difficult to single out individual holes at Ben Slimane, but first timers always remember the eighth, a 180 metre tricky par three; the green being situated on a charming little island, planted with papyrus, requires an accurate and dramatic tee shot to avoid a watery grave.

Natural springs abound and much use has been made of them. Water hazards are numerous and often the golfer is asked to play over or across the edge of a small lake. The rough is rarely punishing, which may not be the case in a few years' time as the course and the rough establishes itself. The bunkers are not too difficult to play out of.

The course is maintained in excellent condition all year round. The fairways are gently undulating and perfectly manicured throughout and the greens are true and have a reputation of being quick. Hundred-year-old cork oaks, pine trees, eucalyptus, and the rough that abounds with flowers, give the course a most attractive appearance.

You will want to return to this challenging, masterpiece of a golf course not only to admire the views but also to get even with it! You are guaranteed a warm and friendly welcome.

# THE SETTAT UNIVERSITY ROYAL GOLF CLUB

Km 2, Route Casablanca

BP 575 Settat

Tel.: (212) 23 40 07 55  (212) 40 07 21

Fax: (212) 23 40 20 99

Par 37

Meters: 3215

Green fees

Holes: 9

75 kilometers from Casablanca, the town of Settat has recently seen transformation from a major agricultural centre to a thriving industrial community. Factories have sprung up, creating employment and bringing prosperity to the area. Employment and industry brings with it a need for special skills, and a scientific and technical university has been established to answer this need. In keeping with the nation's passion for golf, The Settat University Royal Golf Club was established as part of the University sports and studies programme, and its nine holes are played by student groups along with club members and visiting tourists.

Designed by Ronald W Fream, situated near the University and around the racecourse, this small but superb course has wide forgiving fairways, large flat greens and few bunkers. It is the scene of numerous competitions and is continually being developed - already a little tester but soon to be turned into a challenging 18-hole championship course.

RABAT

# RABAT

The fourth of the imperial cities, Rabat is the capital of Morocco, with more than one million inhabitants (the city of Sale north of Rabat, functions as a suburb). Rabat is situated on the Atlantic Ocean, at the mouth of the Bou Regreg estuary, which divides it from Sale. Silting problems have diminished the city's role as a port, but it supports important textile industries. Rabat's industries include the manufacture of textiles, processed food and building materials. Tourism is also an important source of income, together with the administration for the rest of the country. Although Rabat is a commercial and administrative centre, it is challenged by the economically more important city of Casablanca, 80 km southwest.

Rabat is an interesting mix of a long history with a very modern present. There have been settlements on the site of Rabat, since ancient times, but its glory days were in the 12th century, when the then sultan used the kasbah (citadel) as a base for campaigns against the Spanish. It was during this time that the city's most famous landmarks sprang up. It became a haven for Muslims driven out of Spain in the early 17th century, but has only been the capital since the days of the French occupation (1912 to 1956). Rabat has many historical monuments and some of Morocco's most important museums. The city is also the home of the main Royal Palace (built 1950). Rabat has a university (established 1957) and other important academic institutions. All the foreign embassies are located in Rabat. This city opens up only slowly to a visitor.

On the first day of your arrival, you will discover that there is a special atmosphere; compared to other Moroccan cities, people are a bit shy and do not start talking to strangers easily. Rabat's ambience comes from the heady mix of Islamic and European influences in fairly equal proportions. For every place of worship, there are three or four European-style cafes.

Strolling around the city, the many gems of the capital of this magical country will become apparent and it is not always as it first appears. Modern Rabat is clean and open, perhaps a bit too open during the summer heat. But around it, there are both old Muslim quarters, as well as the fascinating remains from all periods of Moroccan history.

Between the city's landmark central park (Jardins Triangle de Vue) and the main train station are most of Rabat's hotels and eating spots. The most obvious cluster of cafes and bars here offer all the beer, kebabs, pizza, olives and ice cream the visitor might need. The Mohammed V international airport is a short ride east of the city and there are plenty of shuttle buses.

## MUST SEE IN RABAT.

## HASSAN TOWER

This uncompleted minaret is the city's most famous site and dominates Rabat's skyline. The Tower Hassan is the 45 metre high minaret of the great mosque begun by Yacoub el-Mansour. The grand building was abandoned when Yacoub el-Mansour died in 1199. The minaret is one of the most beautiful and if completed, it would have been 80m high.

Alongside is the burial site of Mohammed V and of King Hassan II. This monument is an important shrine for Moroccans and one that non-Muslims are permitted to visit. All the traditional Moroccan arts and materials have been utilised in this modern mausoleum - tile, marble, precious stones and brass all worked to perfection.

## ROYAL PALACE

The royal palace lies right in the heart of Rabat. A visitor can approach quite close to the palace before the guards start to get uneasy, but the external appearance belies the beauty behind the walls.

## KASBAH DES OUDAIAS

The Kasbah des Oudaias is built on a bluff overlooking the Atlantic Ocean.

The main entrance to this enclave is through Bab al-Kasbah, otherwise called the Oudaia gate, a glorious example of decorative stone carving from the end of the 12th century. The Kasbah's main street leads past iron-studded house doors and the oldest mosque in Rabat, to the open cannon and semaphore platform. This provides panoramic views over the ocean, the river and the town of Sale on its opposite bank.

The restored 17th-century former palace is now a museum of traditional art.

## THE MEDINA

This is the medina for beginners! Unlike the mazes of some other cities, Rabat's old town follows a grid pattern of straight streets where it is difficult to lose your way. Another advantage is that the merchants are low key. There is no shortage of local colour. The shopping includes silk embroidery, jewellery, brightly coloured Rabat carpets, copperware, and leather.

## CHELLAH

The walled necropolis, from the Merenid dynasty, is a fortress called Chellah. It was built in the 14th century, more or less over the ruins of the ancient Roman colony of Sala. This fascinating site is entered by a gate flanked by two semi-octagonal towers. The stairway descends into lush tropical gardens, with the remains of the Roman site and a sacred pool.

Further on are the Merenid buildings, a roofless mosque with a crumbled minaret and the royal tombs, of which the most impressive are the tombs of Abu Hassan and of his wife, Shams ed-Douna.

## HILTON RABAT

5 Star de Luxe Hotel.

BP 450 - Souissi, Rabat

Tel (212) (37) 67 56 56

Fax (212) (37) 67 40 39

e-mail : rabathilton@mtds.com

Web site: www.hilton.com

This wonderful, top class hotel is highly recommended by the author and is a must for the discerning guest. Excellent service, friendly, efficient staff and great restaurants make this Hotel a golfers paradise complete with superb Health Spa facilities to ease those sore muscles after a round of Golf. It is also ideally located near the Golf Course and has excellent golf practice facilities and a free shuttle service to The Dar Es-Salam Golf Course for guests. Is there anything else one needs?

There are 269 spacious and very comfortable guestrooms all with balconies having superb views, private bathroom, satellite TV. Telephone, mini-bar and air conditioning. There is a piano bar and a patio coffee shop. Delicious dishes are there to tempt you at one of the three excellent restaurants: the gastronomic Le Scalini, the Moroccan Dar Al Andalous and the Mediterranean La Terrazza, with a splendid sunny terrace overlooking the delightful Andalusian gardens.

For a perfect harmony of the body and soul, enjoy the larger outdoor swimming pool of the Hiltonia Club.

# RECOMMENDED

## PLACES TO STAY

**Hotel Tour Hassan – 5 \***
Centrally located.
26 Avenue du Chellah
Tel (212) (37)70 42 02 Fax
(212) (37) 73 18 66
N.B. Free shuttle to Dar Es
Salam Golf Course for guests

**Hôtel Sofitel Diwan – 4\***
Place de l'Unité Africaine
Tel (212) (37) 26 27 27 / Fax
(212) (37) 26 24 24

### RYADS

**Dar Al Batoul**
7 Derb Jirari – Médina
Tel/Fax (212) (37) 72 72 50
e-mail : albatoul@iam.net.ma

**Riad Oudayas**
46 Rue Sidi Fateh – Médina
Tel (212) (37) 70 23 92
e - m a i l :
sandrine.duclos@wanadoo.fr

### BOUTIQUE HOTEL
Villa Mandarine
19 Rue Ouled Bousbaa –
Souissi
Tel (212) (37) 75 20 77 / Fax
(212) (37) 63 23 09

# RECOMMENDED

## PLACES TO EAT

### MOROCCAN CUISINE

**Dar Al Andalous**
Hilton Hotel
Telephone: 212 37 67 56 56

**Dinarjat**
6 Rue Belgnaoui
Tel (212) (37) 70 42 39

### FRENCH CUISINE

**Chez Paul**
82 Ave des Nations Unies
Tel (212) (37) 67 20 00
Fax (212)(37) 67 24 00

**L'entrecôte**
74 Charia Al Amir Fal Ould
oumeir – Agdal
Tel (212) (37) 67 11 08
Fax (212) (37) 67 11 08

**Le puzzle**
79 Ave Ibn Sina – Agdal
Tel (212) (37) 67 00 30
Fax (212) (37) 67 41 44

**Le Provençal**
Ave Hassan II
Témara (15 Km south of
Rabat by the coastal road)
Tel (212) (37) 74 11 11

**L' Eperon Restaurant**
8 Avenue D'Alger
Tel 037 72 59 01
Fax 037 70 76 31

### ITALIAN / MEXICAN CUISINE

**Le Scalini Restaurant**
Hilton Hotel
Telephone 212 37 67 56 56

**La Mamma**
6 Rue Tanta
Tel (212) (37) 70 73 29

**El Rancho**
30 Rue Michlifen – Agdal
Tel (212) (37) 67 33 00

### ASIAN CUISINE

**Fuji**
2 ave Michlifen – Agdal
Tel (212) (37) 67 35 83

**Délices d'Asie**
17 Rue Oqbah – Agdal
Tel (212) (37) 77 94 79

### DISCOTHEQUES

Amnesia
18 Rue Monastir

5° Avenue
4 Ave Bin El Ouidane

## GOLF COURSES IN AND AROUND RABAT

Golf Courses in and Around Casablanca are also within easy reach
if you are based in Rabat.

The Royal Dar Es Salam

Bouznika Bay Golf and Leisure Complex

# THE DAR ES-SALAM ROYAL GOLF CLUB

Dar Es- Salam Rabat

Tel.: (212) (37) 75 58 64/65

Fax: (212) (37) 75 76 71

This championship course is the country's greatest and most beautiful. The course and the surrounding landscape abound with wildlife. A pair of nesting Canadian Fish Eagles can be seen fishing on the lake at the 12th hole, making a spectacular memory. It is also ranked in the top fifty finest courses in the world. Without doubt, it is one of the most challenging with shrubbery, trees and numerous lakes to be negotiated.

Ten minutes from the city centre, the 45 holes at the Royal Dar Es-Salam Golf Club are the dream of golfers from all over the world. This picturesque and beautifully kept 45-hole course was carved out of an ancient cork and eucalyptus forest. It provides excellent golf in a uniquely privileged environment. The famed architect, Robert Trent Jones, gave full rein to his imagination when designing this course, not only preserving, but enhancing the natural beauty of the setting by introducing exotic trees and flowering plants.

Red course

Par 73

Meters: 6702

Holes: 18

Caddies essential

Closed Mondays

Blue course

Par 72

Meters: 6205

Holes: 18

Caddies essential

Closed mondays

Green course

Par 32

Meters: 2150

Holes: 9

Caddies essential

Closed mondays

His Majesty King Hassan II endowed the Capital of the Kingdom with this wonderful facility. Since its opening in 1971, it has hosted all the major international tournaments organised in Morocco: the Hassan II Trophy for professionals, the Hassan II Challenge for amateur players, being the most famous.

## THE RED COURSE

must count as one of Robert Trent Jones' greatest works. It measures a lengthy 6,702 metres (7,329 yards) and constitutes a real test of golf. It calls for precise shot making and there is every chance that, at the end of the round, the golfers will have to use all 14 clubs, in their bag. Only hardened professionals can come up to the par of 73 strokes.

The glorious setting of this magnificent course has been described as both "heavenly" and "hauntingly beautiful". Certainly, walking the fairways, as they wind their way through hundreds of cypress, palm, eucalyptus, cork and oak trees, there is an almost spiritual feeling of peace and tranquillity.

Individual holes are not likely to be easily remembered the first time playing, especially as one will probably be walking the course in a semi-trance. All the holes, however, are a sheer delight and works of art. Accurate drives are essential to avoid trouble in the trees. In addition to the many bunkers, there is water to be negotiated on at least 5 holes.

The image of the wooden bridge, leading to the green of the 9th hole, often photographed for golf books and magazines all around the world, has made this the signature hole of a great golf course. It is a fairly long carry of 172 metres (188 yards) played over the heads of the water lilies. A loose shot will land you in the pond.

Water is also a hazard along the 481 metres (527 yards) of the 12th, closing off the angles to its green. The line of picturesque Roman columns came from the ancient city of Volubilis, near Meknes.

Immediately apparent on reaching the Greens, is the quality of the putting surfaces at Royal Dar Es-Salam – undoubtedly amongst the best in Morocco.

**THE BLUE COURSE:**

Golfers may also wish to investigate the Club's second course. These 18 holes par 72 course are not as demanding as the Red Course but it again must rank as being the most enchanting. White daisies, beds of wild flowers, pink, orange and red, carpets of violet blooms: the fairways have a pastoral charm.

The 11th is the signature hole. A sublime par 4 hides a plateau green nestling between clumps of eucalyptus, a bunker of red sand and a pond with a population of water hens. You cannot take anything for granted - the Blue Course can still surprise you.

## THE GREEN COURSE:

Fewer surprises and a greater feeling of being at ease on this relaxing 9-hole par 32 course, consisting of only par 3 and par 4 holes, which are essentially designed for beginners honing their skills or a quick lunch-time round. Don't let yourself be distracted by the white ox-peckers with orange bills, following every stroke of your play!

Most golfers visiting The Royal Dar Es-Salam Golf club will return home contented, taking with them happy memories of what is unquestionably one of the world's most pleasurable and extraordinary golf courses.

## THE CLUB HOUSE.

The magnificently appointed Clubhouse is a typical sixties building, with clean clear lines, large picture windows and spacious rooms. The members are fortunate in having a wonderfully intimate atmosphere, with an excellent restaurant and bar service.

There is practice green and a practice area. Golf buggies and sets of golf clubs can be hired from the professional. Other amenities include: Tennis courts, outdoor swimming pools, fitness centre, sauna, jacuzzi, gym, hairdresser.

## BOUZNIKA BAY

Tel.: (212) (37) 74 55 55 / (37) 74 33 72

Fax: (212) (37) 74 33 73

Par 35

Meters: 3041

Green fees

Holes: 9

Caddy available

This little course has an ideal location on the coast just a 40 minute drive from the centre of Rabat, in one of the country's finest beach resort communities. It comprises a superb complex with facilities for three areas of activity, beach sports, water sports and golf.

The course was designed by the well-known golf architect Robert Von Hagge and has opened with 9 holes laid around Oued Bouznika, facing the sea. It is one of the two floodlit courses in the country. Bouznika Bay golf course has a state-of-the-art watering system, so is always in pristine condition; the scalloped bunkers are filled with pure white sand and the manicured greens and fairways appear like silk carpets. There are plans to expand into an 18-hole championship course.

The green-keeping staff will point out to visitors and take pride
in the fact that this course is probably one of the best maintained
in Morocco. Always striving for perfection, you will not find a
stone in the bunker out of place, nor a blade of grass not cut to
regulation length in the fringe, the semi or the rough. The greens
are like velvet.

It boasts excellent practice facilities and an impressive modern
Clubhouse with full catering facilities, which are only available
at the weekends.

EL JADIDA

# EL JADIDA

## SOFITEL El JADIDA ROYAL GOLF CLUB

Km 7 Route de Casablanca

Tel.: (212) 23 35 22 51 / 52

(212) 23 35 34 73

Fax: (212) 23 35 41 50

Par 72

Meters: 6539

Holes: 18

Day tickets

Caddies compulsory

Club cars available for hire

Open every day

## GOLFERS PARADISE

Built in 1993, this resort provides nothing but golf, excellent accommodation, rest, recreation, relaxation and good food, especially excellent local fish from the Atlantic. 8 km from El Jadida, El Jadida Royal Golf Club and Hotel is destined to be ranked as one of the great golfing resorts of the world. It has a beautiful, natural setting, with fragrant pines, eucalyptus, tamarisk and mimosa, a lake, sea and a beach.

Cabell B. Robinson designed this 18 hole course to be grandiose: a place where the challenge of golf takes on the beauty of nature. The fragrance of pine and eucalyptus is wafted on the sea breezes. The magnificent araucarias stand like rows of strange vegetable sculptures along the fairways.

The first part of the course is a parkland, the second has a distinctly links flavour. The closing holes are perhaps the only ones which have true traditional links features.

There are several tee positions on each hole that change the outline of the course to suit individual requirements. The 3rd is a good contemporary hole, requiring two firm blows, (the second avoiding the water) theoretically finding a narrow, angled and heavily contoured green that can be impossible to hold with a pitch. The 16th is the signature hole of this magnificent course: 182 meters, a classic par 3 with an outstanding view of the sea from an elevated tee. It requires a good knock into the wind to make it to this tiered green.

Standing on the 18th tee, a view of the welcoming clubhouse in the distance, the sound of the waves breaking in the background, seagulls flying in perfect formation above the Atlantic surf, and the setting sun, this is a spectacle impossible to match anywhere in the golfing world.

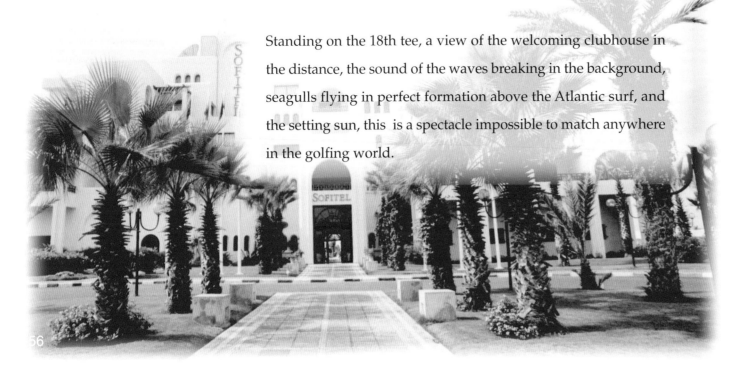

The practice and putting facilities are some of the best in the country. The Sofitel Hotel acts as a rather grand 19th. An excellent and very full range of catering is offered; additional light snacks are available throughout the day in the new golfer's bar. But the balcony terrace, with its panoramic views over the course and surrounding Hotel gardens is a must on a warm day - imagine sitting out there on a bright and clear day with just a hint of breeze and a cool drink in your hand and the sound of waves breaking on the shore in the distance.

There are over 125 rooms and suites at this Golf Resort Hotel, each with balcony or terrace, and each affording superb views of the sea, gardens or pool. All rooms have air-conditioning, bathroom, safe, telephone, satellite TV and mini-bar.

The hotel offers a choice of restaurants: the 'Le Mazagan' restaurant serving international cuisine, the 'Al Jawhara' Moroccan restaurant, the Club House 'Birdie' snack bar, and the relaxing Piano Bar. The hotel's facilities include a large swimming pool, with separate children's area, two tennis courts, conference facilities and a health and fitness centre. Horse-riding can be arranged less than four miles away at the El Jadida Equestrian Club.

TANGIER

# TANGIER

Tangier is a leisurely 3 hour drive from Rabat and well served by train connections to the rest of the country.  It is also an easy ferry ride from Spain or Gibraltar and has been called the Gateway to Morocco.   Overlooking the Straits of Gibraltar with a view of Spain's southern coast, it is situated on a spectacular bay.

Tangier has always been a magnet for travellers throughout history. In the 14th Century, it became a major Mediterranean port frequented by European trading vessels bringing cloth, spices, metals and hunting birds in exchange for leather, wool, carpets, cereals and sugar.

The Portuguese conquered and occupied the city in 1471, converting the great mosque into a cathedral. For nearly three centuries the town was passed back and forth between the Spanish and the Portuguese.  Finally it fell into the hands of the English, when it was given to Charles II as part of the dowry of Catherine of Braganza. The English granted Tangier a charter, which gave the city equal status to that of English towns.

In the 17th Century Moulay Ismail  saw the British off, but before they left they rather unsportingly  destroyed the town and its port facilities.  Under Moulay Ismail the city was reconstructed to some extent, but it gradually fell into decline until, by 1810, the population was no more than 5,000.

Ironically, Tangier began to revive during the mid-19th century when European colonial governments fought for influence over Morocco. France, Spain, England and Germany jockeyed for position in Tangier where most diplomatic missions were located.

The Algeciras Conference in 1906, attended by all the European powers, granted Tangier a special status as 'The Tangier Zone'. This placed the town and its surrounding territory under the authority of an International Commission, with the Sultan of Morocco as nominal ruler.

A protocol, signed in 1925 by Great Britain, France, and Spain, provided for permanent security of the city. However, in 1929 Spain was given police powers and Tangier was placed under the legislative control of an international body.

During World War II Tangier was completely controlled by Spain, reverting to international authority in 1945. With independence in 1956, Tangier became a fully integrated part of the Kingdom of Morocco.

It is still an international city; a meeting place of cultures and an inspiration to writers and artists, unique in Morocco for its tolerance and cosmopolitan flavour.

## PLACES OF INTEREST

### THE GRAND SOCCO

The Grand Socco, or the big souk, is one of the traditional centres of Tangier life. From here you walk through an archway into the medina, a bustling hillside with a maze of winding streets and lanes in which artisans of different trades —woodworkers, jewellers, shoemakers — congregate.

### THE PETIT SOCCO

The city's central Petit Socco or little souk is a pleasant open space with several cafes. Back in the days when Tangier was a neutral international zone, this area provided the background for the seediest of lifestyles and this atmosphere has not been completely lost. All Tangier still passes by — businessmen in striped jellabas, women in kaftans or couture outfits, playful children and, of course, tourists.

### THE KASBAH

The Kasbah, a citadel since Roman times, lies at the top of the hill above the medina. This fortress was the centre of administration for old Tangier. Here Moulay Ismail chose to build his Palace, behind the batteries of cannon installed on the walls. The Sultan's Garden, part of Moulay Ismail's 17th Century palace, is just beyond a large unmarked doorway in Rue Riad Sultan. From the fragrant garden you enter the sultan's palace, Dar el Makhzen, now a Museum of Moroccan Art. This houses all manner of treasures, from illuminated Korans to wood and metal work, as well as Berber carpets and a collection of ceramics. The palace itself is a work of art, with its two richly decorated courtyards.

## FORBES MUSEUM

The unconventional American magazine publisher, Malcolm Forbes, restored and maintained a residence in the Mendoub Palace in Rue Shakespeare. He died in 1990 and left a record-breaking collection of toy soldiers, many deployed to illustrate notable battles, in the Forbes Museum of Military Miniatures. The Palace gardens are lovely with splendid views over the sea.

## NEW TOWN

Leading south from the Grand Socco, the Rue de la Liberte goes to the centre of the modern city of Tangier — Place de France and Boulevard Pasteur. Cafes, restaurants, travel agencies and bookstores are all within a few streets, and there is a fine panoramic view of the harbour, looking towards the Spanish mainland.

## CAP SPARTEL - OLD LIGHTHOUSE

A few miles due west of Tangier the old lighthouse marks the most northwestern point in Africa. It stares out at the supertankers sailing between the Atlantic and the Mediterranean. You can climb the spiral staircase to the observation level.

# RECOMMENDED

# PLACES TO STAY

**Mövenpick – 5***
22 Rue Malabata Bella Vista
Contact: Samira Ktira
Tel: (212) (39) 340534
Fax: (2120 (39) 340548
Email:
hotel.tangier@movenpick.co.
ma

**Le Mirage – 5***
Tel: (212) (39) 33 33 32
Fax: (212) (39) 33 34 92
Email : mirage@iam.net.ma
Open : April through
November.

**El Minzah – 5***
85 Rue de la Liberté
Tel (212) (39) 93 58 85
Fax (212) (39) 93 45 46
Email :
elminzah@tangeroise.net.ma

# RECOMMENDED

# PLACES TO EAT

## Moroccan cuisine

**Moroccan restaurant of the El Minzah Hotel (« El Korsan »)**

**Mamounia Palace**
6 Rue Semmarine
Tel (212) (39) 93 50 99

**Restaurant Michlifen**
15 Rue Moulay Abdellah
Tel (212) (39) 93 13 31

## International Cuisine

**London's Pub**
15 Rue Mansour Ad-Dahbi
Tel (212) (39) 94 20 94

**The Pub**
4 Rue Sorolla
Tel (212) 39) 93 47 89

**Restaurant Las Conchas**
30 Rue Ahmed Chaouki
Tel (212) (39) 93 16 43

## Italian Cuisine

**Casa d'Italia**
In the Moulay Hafid Palace

**Restaurant San Remo**
15 Rue Ahmed chaouki
Tel (212) (39) 93 84 51

## Sea food and Spanish cuisine

**Restaurant Romero**
12 Ave Prince Moulay Abdellah
Tel (212) (39) 93 22 77

**Restaurant Valencia**
Ave Youssef Ibn Tachfine

**Restaurant of Hotel « Le Mirage »**
Tel (212) (39) 33 33 31

## GOLF COURSES IN AND AROUND

## TANGIER

Royal Country Club of Tangier

Cabo Negro Royal Golf Club

# ROYAL COUNTRY CLUB OF TANGIER

BP 41, Tangier

Tel.: 212 (39) 93 89 25

Fax: 212 (39) 93 9025 / 94 3803

Year opened 1917

Par 70

Meters: 5545

Yards: 6046

Holes: 18

Green fees

Caddies available

Open daily

The Royal Golf Club of Tangier is situated four kilometres southwest of Tangier and ten minutes from the city centre. This was the first golf course in Morocco, established by the British community on land donated by King Moulay Abdelaziz, who also inaugurated it in 1917.

Ever since this 18-hole course has undergone regular improvements to become one of Morocco's finest, while retaining its own very special style. Two British golf architects, Pennink and Cotton, take the credit for the present 18-hole layout.

It can be described as a typical English parkland course set in a combination of valley and hills. The course starts off by the sea, clings to the hillside and then sweeps down into a forest of fir, pine cypress and eucalyptus, before rising once more. It has gently bending tree-lined fairways, flat old-fashioned bunkers and large, raised greens as well as sporting a splendid view over the city and bay of Tangier.

Although not a championship course, it is nevertheless testing. As with seaside courses all over the world, the vagaries of the wind must always be considered. The golfer does not come to The Royal Tangier to seek golf's toughest challenge, but will enjoy the splendour of a unique setting.

The 19th - as one comes to expect in Morocco, is exceptionally helpful and friendly. The newly built and delightful clubhouse has a roof of green tiles. The welcoming veranda looks out over a large garden with a fountain and also overlooks the putting green and the practice area. The clubhouse offers some of the finest dining in Morocco.
The club has a minimal playing membership and visitors are received warmly.

Year opened 1976

18 holes

Par 72

6120 meters

Green fees

Caddies available

Open daily.

## CABO NEGRO ROYAL GOLF CLUB

BP 696 G. Tetouan

Tel.: 212 (39) 97 81 41

Fax: 212 (39) 97 83 05

Close to a charming seaside resort and about 45 minutes from Tangier, behind Tetouan and the summits of the Rif, lies the Royal Golf Club of Cabo Negro. A remarkable golf course which was originally conceived and designed by Martin Hawtree in 1976 as an 18 hole course, but left uncompleted. It was then remodelled by Cabell B. Robinson.

Cabo Negro will not wear you out, but it will definitely challenge you to play some precise approach shots to the green. The course has wide, open fairways, large gently rolling greens and shallow simple bunkers. Robinson has made magnificent use of the landscape and some of the short holes he created here, are among the most seductive in Morocco. The 3rd is the most talked about; it is a 180 meter par 3 over water. The tee shot must be measured to perfection to avoid not only the water but also the devilishly positioned bunkers guarding the green.

The pure white sand is abundant everywhere on the course, as are the agaves and mimosas.

There is a pleasant clubhouse with a large thatched roof set in the shade of a mimosa tree, with a view of the putting green, the 9th and the sea beyond. There are plans for a luxury hotel to be constructed nearby, offering a whole range of sporting and leisure pursuits. In time, this site will become a perfect sporting holiday destination.

FÉS

74

This old imperial city is easily reached by train or car from Rabat, Marrakesh or Tangier.

## FES

In A.D. 789, Idriss I  began to create the nucleus of a new Islamic city, which was later developed into a stunning capital by his son , the great Moroccan ruler saint Moulay Idris II. Subsequent dynasties embellished Fes with world famous monuments, hundreds of palaces, grand buildings, mosques, shrines, academic institutions and fortifications.

The city is situated in a narrow valley against the backdrop of the Middle Atlas.  It is strategically positioned on the old crossroads of caravan routes connecting the Saharan empires, like Timbuktu and Takrur, with the Atlantic and the Mediterranean shipping lanes.

The oldest and most ravishing of the imperial cities, the symbolic heart of Morocco, Fes remained the power centre and capital of Morocco until the 16th Century. Over a thousand years of political, spiritual, intellectual, cultural and commercial superiority is reflected in the people of Fes, who are famous for their self assurance and sophistication.

Fes remained a commercial centre for much of its history. It is still considered Morocco's premier religious city by virtue of its great Islamic traditions. It is the site of the Karaouine Mosque and is also the burial place of Moulay Idris II. Apart from the European town built after World War II, Fes is divided into two distinct areas: Fes el Jdid (the new) and Fes el Bali (the old). Textile and flourmills, oil-processing plants, tanneries, soap factories, and a large handicraft industry all can be found within the city of Fes.

Many people have moved from the older imperial city to the modern suburbs, but the ancient city is powerfully compelling and it remains one of the world's great architectural treasures.

## PLACES OF INTEREST

### FES EL BALI

This is the oldest and most exotic part of the city. It is the largest, inhabited medieval city in the world; the gates and walls that surround it make it all the more magnificent.

Experience the sights and smell of the medina, whilst mingling with ordinary people going about their business. There are thousands of winding streets and hundreds of craftsmen and artisans, in mini communities, plying their wares, including the famous henna souk, a market specialising in the dye used for colouring hair and tattooing women's hands and feet.

Donkeys are still the main carriers of loads here. Shopping is particularly good for carpets and ornate metalwork.

Towering over the medina is one of the country's outstanding monuments - Medersa Bou Inania, a theological college built in 1350.

A local guide is recommended when visiting the medina, as it is easy to get lost.

## FES JDID

The Merenid sultans built Fes Jdid outside the walls of the Fes El Bali. The site dates from the 13th Century and is dominated by the Royal Palace (closed to visitors) and the old Jewish quarter (the mellah).

## THE VILLE NOUVELLE

This is the new town dating from the French era and is the centre of commerce. Here the populace congregates for the early evening promenade along the broad avenues, punctuated by stops for mint tea at the outdoor cafes.

## TOMB OF MOULAY IDRIS II

Considered one of the most sacred places in all of Morocco, the tomb of Moulay Idris II is a place of pilgrimage for Muslims from throughout Morocco and the Islamic world. The superb interiors are richly ornamented. Non-Muslims may not enter or even draw near the entrance.

## KARAOUINE MOSQUE

One of the largest mosques in Africa, the Karaouine Mosque is also one of the world's most beautiful places of worship. For over a thousand years, great Muslim saints and scholars have congregated in its ornamental courtyard. It remains one of the most majestic monuments of Islam.

# RECOMMENDED

## PLACES TO STAY

**Hôtel Palais Jamaï – 5***
Bab Guissa
Tel 212) (55) 63 43 31
Fax (212) (55) 63 50 96

**Hôtel Jnan Palace – 5***
Ave Ahmed Chaouki
Tel (212) (55) 65 22 30 / 65 39 65
Fax (212) (55) 65 19 17

**Hôtel Méridien Mérinides – 5***
Borj Nord
Tel (212) (55) 64 52 26 / 64 62 18
Fax (121) (55) 64 52 25

## RYADS

**La Maison Bleue**
2 Place de l'Istiqlal, Batha
Tel (212) (55) 63 60 / 74 06 86
Fax (212) (55) 74 18 43

# RECOMMENDED

## PLACES TO EAT

### Moroccan cuisine

Moroccan restaurants of most hotels

**Palais de Fes**
16 Rue Bou-Touil Karaouiyne
Tel (212) (55) 63 47 07

**Dar Fassia**
Hotel Palais Jamai Restaurant

**Palais Mnebhi**
15 Souikat Ben Safi
Tel (212) (55) 63 38 93

**La Maison Bleue**
2 place de l'Istiqlal – Batha
Tel (212) (55) 63 60 52

**Palais Vizir**
39 Znikt Hajjama
Tel (212) (55) 63 61 83

### Italian and international cuisine

**Chez Vittorio**
21 Rue Brahim Roudani
Tel (212) (55) 62 47 30

**La Cheminée**
6 Ave Lalla Asmaa
Tel (212) (55) 62 49 02

**Assouan**
4 Ave Allal Ben Abdelah
Tel (212) (55) 62 51 50

# FÉS ROYAL GOLF CLUB

Route d'Ifrane-Imouzzer-Aïn Chegag

Tel: 212 (55) 66 52 10

Fax: 212 (55) 65 19 17

Situated 14 km from Fes, this is a beautiful 9 hole gem.  It is sited 3 km from the airport and 2 hours drive from Rabat.

The course is carved out of a magnificent olive grove. It has a peaceful and tranquil countryside setting with views of the Atlas mountains. Once again, Cabell B. Robinson has come up trumps, creating an exquisite and imaginatively sculpted golf course in a majestic setting, accentuating the natural contours of the terrain to produce the undulating fairways, preserving the natural flora and fauna and creating the tricky sloping greens – the trade mark of The Fes Royal Golf Course.

The course is typically American, with wide open fairways, multiple tee positions, bunkers, giant bunkers and monumental bunkers and, of course, water. There are five lakes creating interesting water hazards, all beautifully blended into the course layout, as only our American friends know how.

Year opened 199

9 hole

Par 3

3168 meter

Green fee

Caddies available

Open daily

The course is immaculate and, refreshingly, not a long hitter's course. The fairway shots to the green are what the Royal Fes Golf Course is all about, with some excellent par fours. Many of the greens have magnificent stage-like settings protected by trees, shrubs, sand and water. The most celebrated hole is perhaps the opening par four, requiring two precise shots to get on. The drive must be perfectly positioned for the approach is downhill to a smallish green guarded by trees on one side and water on the other. The fourth is also a par 4 and a real test of precision play to avoid a watery grave on the left and the right.

Another feature of The Royal Fes Golf Course is the remarkable variety of wildlife, which the golfer is likely to come across, especially the more wayward hitter. The round concludes with some very testing holes.

The clubhouse is majestic and houses framed photographs of the late King with his young sons during their many Royal Golfing Rounds at this delightful little course. The views from the terraces of the clubhouse over this lush course and surrounding countryside will be etched into your memory for life.

When the course is fully opened with 18 holes, complete with a luxury hotel, it will be a magnet for golfers looking for that little extra from their golfing holiday.

MEKNES

## MEKNES

Easily accessible and with a population of around 750,000, Meknes is called the Moroccan Versailles. Sultan Moulay Ismail built this imperial city as the Moroccan capital, on a fertile plain north of the Middle Atlas near Fes.

Moulay Ismail came to power in 1672, aged 26, and reigned for 55 years. When a French princess refused his hand in marriage, the young Sultan swore that he would build a palace that would rival Versailles in splendour. He pressed 50,000 workers into service building a series of palaces, mile after mile of walls, battlements and ramparts, and a vast marketplace. The imperial city was completed by Moulay Ismail's son, Moulay Abdallah (1727-1757), and his grandson, Sidi Mohamed ben Abdallah (1757-1790). In the early 19th century, Meknes ceased to be an imperial capital and became neglected. It was not until the reign of Moulay Hassan, at the end of the century, that Meknes was restored and revived enough to testify to a magnificent dream.

The surrounding region is fertile and the city produces many agricultural products including fruit, grain and vegetables, as well as metalwork, carpets, woollen fabrics and cement. The Roman ruins of Volubilis and the holy city of Moulay Idriss, established in A.D. 788, where the founder of Morocco is buried, are located to the north.

## PLACES OF INTEREST

### BAB EL MANSOUR DOOR

Famed as the finest gateway in North Africa, the monumental Bab Mansour has become the symbol of Meknes. Named after the architect, a Christian slave converted to Islam, the symmetry of the enormous edifice is pleasing. Take the time to absorb the intricacies of the decorations above the main horseshoe arch and the smaller side arches of the bastions. (Among the inscriptions, in graceful calligraphy, is praise for Moulay Ismail and his son, Moulay Abdallah, who finished the construction.)

### MAUSOLEUM

Moulay Ismail did not forget to build his own last resting place. Pilgrims, especially country folk, still come to this lavish mausoleum to pray in the memorial mosque.

### THE MEDINA

Less mysterious than the souks of Fes and Marrakech, this is one of the easiest medinas to explore without a guide. Artisans produce everything from carpet slippers to saddles. You can see a carpet being woven or a table sanded and polished. All the fragrances of the orient are here, and goods on sale range from saffron in giant sacks to skewered meat sizzling on the grill.

## MOULAY IDRISS

In this white-walled town north of Meknes lies the tomb of a great grandson of the Prophet Mohammed, the sultan-saint Moulay ldris, founder of the first Moroccan Arab dynasty.

## VOLUBILIS

About 20 miles from the city of Meknes, is the site of the largest and best preserved Roman ruins in Morocco. Volubilis dates largely from the 2nd and 3rd centuries A.D., although excavations have revealed that the site was originally settled even earler by Carthaginian traders. There is a hotel nearby.

# RECOMMENDED

## PLACES TO STAY

**Hotel Rif. Rue Zankat Accra**

Telephone 522591 Fax 524428,

A huge and typical city hotel. Swimming pool, restaurant, bar and air conditioned throughout. The hotel organises city tours to Volubilis and Moulay ldris.

**Hotel Transatlantique Rue El Merinyine**

Telephone: 525050 Fax 520057

Luxury Hotel. One of those places where you can imagine you are back in the old colonial days. There are two pools, tennis courts and extensive gardens with views over the medina. Rooms with air conditioning and all other creature comforts. Excellent bar.

# RECOMMENDED

## PLACES TO EAT

### Medina

There are a few simple restaurants along Rue Dar Smen. Two of the best are:

**Restaurant Economique** at No 123

**Restaurant Bab Mansour** at No 127

### Moroccan and International

**Collier de la Colombe** (tel: 55041, 67 Rue Driba). Unparalleled view over the river.

**Hotel Transatlantique.** Serves old-fashioned Moroccan food.

### French

**Hacienda** telephone 52109. 2 miles outside Meknes on the Fes Road. A good French restaurant, with bar, dancing and al-fresco dining.

# MEKNES ROYAL GOLF CLUB

Year opened 1971

9 holes

Par 36

2707 meters

Green fees

Caddies available

Open daily.

Bab Belkari Jnane Lbahraouia,

Meknes

Tel.: 212 (55) 53 07 53

Fax: 212 (55) 55 79 34

The Meknes Royal Golf Club is a picturesque nine-hole course, rooted deep in history. It is situated in the heart of the imperial city of the Sultan Moulay Ismaïl, the roofs and minarets of the medina forming a marvellous background. The course is laid out within the walled gardens of the Royal Palace behind the high battlements and in the middle of a magnificent Andalusian style garden, overflowing with flowers, plum, orange, palm, olive and apricot trees. This is a setting unique in the golfing world, complete with ramparts, a fountain covered with mosaics, sculpted windows and niches, colonnades and towers. A huge ancient intricately carved arched wooden door forms the imposing entrance to the Club.

It is not a difficult course, but playing it is a fascinating adventure into the history of this ancient and beautiful imperial city. Close to the 4th green, a Moorish door leads into the Royal Palace. Outside the walls and six metres away from the 6th green, lie the remains of the great Sultan Moulay Ismail.

The rough along with the bushes, plants and trees are so well tended by the green keepers that it is impossible to lose your ball. The fairways or rather lawns are ornamented with a profusion of flowers.

Off the 7th green, an exquisite staircase in white and green earthenware leads to the ramparts where the clubhouse is situated. The offices and changing rooms lie within the walls, along with a welcoming clubhouse lounge. This offers an unparalleled view onto the course and its magnificent architectural surroundings. There is a shady terrace for that long cool, after round drink, soaking up the atmosphere and transporting yourself back in time.

The enchantment lasts throughout the round, and even into the night if you so desire, for here you can play by both floodlight and moonlight.

AGADIR

On February 29th 1960, an earthquake completely destroyed the old city of Agadir. The nation rallied and a new city was built on safe flatlands south of the danger zone, 310 miles southwest of Casablanca,

Agadir boasts an excellent selection of golf courses, hotels of all categories, a beautiful beach, year-round sunshine, legendary Moroccan hospitality, a tremendous range of leisure facilities, night clubs, restaurants - all this and more, only three hours flying time from Europe - a golfer's paradise indeed! Extremely popular with Europeans, this international resort has recently begun to be discovered by Americans.

The evenings bring difficult choices among the shops, the international restaurants, cafes and late night discos. All these assets and a new international airport make Agadir the number one tourist town in Morocco, the sort of resort where they have a menu printed in your language, no matter which language you speak.

The centre of the new city is a noisy hustle and bustle of concrete, commerce and traffic, but there are pedestrian malls and parks to relieve the urban stress, and an aviary called the Valley of the Birds. Beyond the business centre, the city planners laid out industrial and residential zones. They reserved the choicest real estate sites, along the bay, for  hotel development, where, as in Las Vegas, the newest hotel is usually bigger and more lavish than its neighbour. The tourist sector expansion goes on for miles, with no end in sight; but, neither is there an end in sight to the glorious beach.

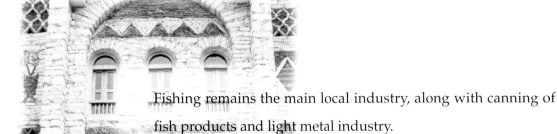

Fishing remains the main local industry, along with canning of fish products and light metal industry.

## PLACES OF INTEREST

### THE KASBAH

Discreet signs point the way to a road, which winds up to the top of a large hill where the ruins of the old town lie. Here also, are the remains of thousands of earthquake victims, within the walls of the old kasbah. The ramparts are essentially all that is left.

There is also a magnificent view of the port, beach and the new city from the hilltop.

### NEW MEDINA

La Medina D'Agadir is a few miles south of Agadir on the Inezgane road. It is a modern medina, a living ethnological museum and a bazaar conceived by a Moroccan-born, Italian architect.

The buildings are made of earth, rock from the Souss, slate from the High Atlas, and local woods and each stone is laid by hand. Decorations follow both Berber and Saharan motifs. Mosaic craftsmen, painters, jewellers, a henna artist, metalworkers, and carpenters practise their crafts and welcome spectators.

# RECOMMENDED

# PLACES TO STAY

**Dorint Atlantic Palace – 5***
BP 194 Secteur Balnéaire
Tel (212) (48) 82 41 46 / Fax (212) (48) 84 43 92

**Beach Club –5***
BP 310
Tel (212) (48) 84 43 43 / Fax (212) (48) 84 08 63

**Tikida Beach Hotel –4***
Chemin des Dunes
Tel (212) (48) 84 54 00 / Fax (212) (48) 84 58 62

# RECOMMENDED

# PLACES TO EAT

## Moroccan Cuisine

Moroccan restaurants of most hotels

**Al Baraka** (in Aourir)
Tel (212) (48) 31 40 74

## ITALIAN CUISINE

**La Siciliana**
Boulevard Hassan II
Tel (212) (48)  82 09 73

**El Paradiso**
Boulevard Mohamed V
Tel (212)(48) 84 83 04

## International and french cuisine

**L'Imprivé
Galeries Tafoukt,**
bd du 20 Août
Tel (212) (48) 84 18 34

**Mimi La Brochette**
Promenade du Bord de Mer, complexe Almoggar
Tel (212) (48) 84 03 87

**Marine Heim**
2 Bd Mohamed V
Tel (212) (48) 84 07 31

## SPECIAL FISH

**Le Miramar**
Bd Mohamed V
Tel (212) (48) 84 07 70

**Restaurant du Port**
(Harbour)
Tel (212) (48) 84 37 08

# AGADIR DUNES GOLF CLUB (27 HOLES)

Golf les Dunes

Chemin Oued Souss

Agadir


Tel: 212 (48) 83 45 47

Fax: 212 (48) 83 46 49

Year opened 1991

27 holes

3 loops of 9 Holes

Yellow 3050 meters Par 36

Blue 3174 meters Par 36

Red 3208 meters Par 36

Green fees

Caddies available

Open daily

Ten minutes drive from the town centre is the Golf Les Dunes, beautifully landscaped to international standards by architect Cabell Robinson, covering 107 hectares: 3 courses 9 holes, par 36. It has a huge driving range in front of the clubhouse, a putting area, a pitching green with bunker practice, a pro-shop, a clubhouse with catering services and a large terrace overlooking the practice area.

Cabell B. Robinson has incorporated a number of remarkable surprises into these three, nine hole, par 36 courses, each with its own special features and difficulties.

However the lovely view, wildlife, undulations of the fairways and the real dunes of all shapes and sizes are common features of all three.

There are seven huge and beautiful lakes with their picturesque fountains. The Dunes Golf Resort is beautifully presented, professionally managed, immaculately kept and the whole complex is a visual delight. Several holes are stunning, all are beautiful. It is quite simply a shatteringly beautiful track, a golfer's dream. The practice facilities must be the best in Morocco, if not Europe.

## THE EUCALYPTUS, THE BLUE COURSE

This is an ideal course for getting your hand in. As the name suggests, these beautiful trees feature strongly and at times they leave very little room for the fairways.

The holes, which might look easy from the elevated tees, unfold traps only when it is too late, thanks to the hundreds and thousands of green dunes. There are surprises on every hole and hole number 8 is a gem, not only in its golfing challenge but also its setting. A narrow fairway winds its way through the trees, with an abrupt shift towards the right in the vicinity of the green, which suddenly comes into view, on the top of a hill surrounded by bunkers. After the flag has been replaced, do spare a few minutes to take in the magnificent, uninterrupted prospect of Inezgane with its whitewashed houses and minarets.

## OUED - THE YELLOW COURSE

This course needs much more skill. Each hole is beautifully laid out, providing a different stunning vista of the surrounding countryside. The tee to hole number 5 is the highest on the course. Up there, on dunes cooled by the Atlantic breeze, you are treated to a most awe-inspiring view, not only of the golf courses but also of the last foothills of the Anti Atlas, and the river Oued Souss flowing towards the Atlantic.

The masterpiece and the signature hole is the 9th. A spectacular hole; whichever way you tackle it, designed to ruin your scorecard! It is a long 513 metres par5, double dog leg around the lake with a very narrow green guarded by sand, lake, deep depression and a huge mound. You could not find a better closing hole to test your composure.

## TAMARISK – THE RED COURSE

For this course, you will need all your clubs and all your best shots. Water dominates this course and in particular the opening holes.

Many of the holes are fairly long, requiring a good drive to stand any chance of getting on in regulation. Here again the finishing hole is magnificent and unexpected. Playing from the very centre of a thick eucalyptus forest, the narrow fairway cuts through the trees climbing and then rolling down gently towards the green and the clubhouse. Accuracy is required to avoid a walk in the woods.

## THE CLUBHOUSE

The clubhouse at the Dunes Golf club is a treat, a building blending modern and traditional features. It has a bright, open airy feel and offers a whole range of first class facilities including a well stocked Pro Shop.

There is an unmistakeably relaxed, holiday flavour about the Dunes. After the game, everybody assembles on the sunny terrace overlooking the practice ground. In keeping with everything else, the catering and bar facilities are excellent. The staff are most pleasant and helpful.

## GOLF DU SOLEIL (27 HOLES)
## GOLF DU SOLEIL RESORT

Chemin Des Dunes

BP 901

Agadir

Tel: 212 (48) 83 73 29 / 30

Fax: 212 (48) 83 73 33

Golf Du Soleil is a superb new 27-hole, international standard, golf facility in Agadir. It is a magnificent, five star plus golf resort, that will surely make Agadir one of the premier golfing destinations in the world.

Year opened 1999

27 holes

3 loops of 9 Holes

Yellow 3011 meters Par 36

Blue 2956 meters Par 36

Red 2969 meters Par 36

Green fees

Rental clubs available

Caddies compulsory

Open daily

Golf du Soleil is located on the Atlantic Coast and was designed by Fernando Muela. He gave full rein to his imagination when shaping this exceptional piece of art. There are three nine-hole courses, all with gently undulating fairways, eucalyptus, tamarisk, mimosa and the palm trees which are ever present at Golf du Soleil, lining just about every fairway and giving the course somewhat of a tropical feel. The greens are quick and treacherously sloping. All three courses are a dream to play on, each offering a variety of golfing challenges. Every hole is magnificent, designed with care and attention to detail, incorporating water, bridges, waterfalls, beautiful indigenous trees, flowering plants and the natural rise and fall of the land, all fanned by the fresh, cooling Atlantic breeze.

The practice facilities are also superb and incorporate a putting green. Individual lessons by a first class resident professional are available and there is a driving range with more than adequate number of bays. Everything here is designed to allow you to concentrate on your favourite game, including an hourly free shuttle service to your hotel.

The clubhouse is spectacular; a marvellous example of Moorish architecture, there is an inherent grandeur and quiet about the place. It also has a relaxed ambience, a panoramic terrace, a well-stocked pro shop, a full service bar, a highly acclaimed restaurant and a huge conference room.

# AGADIR ROYAL GOLF CLUB (09 HOLES)

## ROYAL GOLF CLUB OF AGADIR

Km 12

Route Ait Melloul

Agadir

Tel: 212 (48) 24 85 51

Fax: 212 (48) 33 55 33

Year opened 1955

9 holes

Par 36

2760 meters

Green fees

Caddies available

Open daily

12 Kilometres from Agadir city centre, on the way to Ait Melloul is situated one of the best known golf courses in Morocco, The Royal Golf Club of Agadir.

Founded in 1955 by two golf enthusiasts, a Scotsman and a Moroccan Army Officer, in what was, at that time, the middle of nowhere. Thanks to the many improvements made over the years, it has become a prestigious Golf Club with a magnificent 9-hole course, soon to be extended to 18.

It is a pleasant parkland course of medium length, not far from the breezes of the ocean. The Royal Agadir is especially famed for its wide fairways, filled with the scent of pines, eucalyptus, geraniums and mimosas that abound on this historic little course. The greens are broad and generally flat, protected by deep bunkers and groups of palm trees that close off the angles. The 3rd hole is particularly challenging; it is a splendid 469 metres Par 5 requiring particular skill on the second shot, to overcome the impressive water hazard.

The Club may have avoided professional tournaments but over the years it has played host to a number of important national amateur tournaments.

A pleasant well-tended garden encompasses the welcoming and informal clubhouse with its large picture windows giving vistas of cooling greenery. A variety of reasonably priced meals are available, served by very helpful and extremely obliging staff.

OUARZAZATE

# OUARZAZATE

An interesting and varied itinerary, combining beach, mountains, an exciting city and golf would be as follows. Fly to Agadir, drive through the Atlas Mountains admiring the breathtaking scenery, to Marrakech. Ouarzazate would be an overnight stop. Ouarzazate, in the Atlas Mountains, is a modern town, administrative capital of the southeast of Morocco, the gateway to the desert. It is an army town with soldiers on bicycles trundling past the carpet salesmen.

Local luxury hotels cater to coachloads of tourists and to international film crews. Year-round sunshine, dunes, camels and low-budget extras have made this town the Hollywood of Africa. Among the famous films shot in Ouarzazate are Lawrence of Arabia, The Sheltering Sky, The Last Temptation of Christ and The Gladiator.

Ouarzazate has an international airport.

## PLACES OF INTEREST

## KASBAH TAOURIRT

Ouarzazate's principal historical monument, at the crest of Avenue Mohammed V, is a kasbah, or feudal family castle. Kasbah Taourirt was built by the Glaoui warlords, who ruled over much of southern Morocco in the 19th Century and well into the 20th. In its heyday, the kasbah housed the many relatives of the chiefs, as well as an army of hangers-on, servants and craftsmen.

Guides lead visitors through restored parts of the complex, the harem quarters being the most interesting. The traditional construction techniques using palm wood, straw and mud, are readily visible.

From the upper storeys, there is a view of the modern El Mansour dam which provides water and electricity to the district. The lake, created by the dam, surrounds an island topped by a ruined kasbah, and provides an unexpected opportunity for swimming or rowing in the midst of a desolate red landscape.

## FILM STUDIOS

If you have a spare hour or two, you might want to visit the sets at the film studios, located a short taxi ride outside the City. With a little bit of plaster, some imagination, a pretty face or two and some costumes, all carefully put on celluloid, you can be anywhere in time or place.

# RECOMMENDED

## PLACES TO STAY

**Hotel Sol Melia Karam**
Ave Moulay Rachid
BP 150
Ouarzazate
Tel 212 (44) 88 22 25
Fax 212 (44) 88 56 42

**Hotel Riad Salem**
Ave. Mohamed V
Tel 212 (44) 88 33 35
Fax 212 (44) 88 27 66 62

**Hotel Berbere Palace**
Rue Mansour Eddahbi
Tel: 212 (44) 88 31 05
Fax 212 (44) 88 30 70

# RECOMMENDED

## PLACES TO EAT

**International and Moroccan**

**Chez Dimitri**
22 Ave. Mohammed V
Telephone: 212 (44) 88 26 53

**Ichbilia (Seville)**
Route de Marrakech (P31)
Tamassint
Telephone: 212 (44) 88 67 21

# ROYAL GOLF CLUB OF OUARZAZATE

BP 83

Ouarzazate

Tel: 212 (44) 88 22 18 / 88 24 86

Fax: 212 (44) 88 25 68

Year opened 1993

9 holes

Par 36

3150 meters

Green fees

Caddies available

Open daily

Do not expect this course to be as professionally maintained and run as the Royal title implies, but there are plans on the table to develop the area and improve and extend this nine-hole course. However, it does have a most remarkable setting - in the middle of nowhere, at the very portals of the desert, at the beginning of the Kasbah trail.

The spectacular High Atlas can be seen from all points on this course. Playing here is both incredibly captivating and complex. The narrow, dry, broken terrain of the fairways with their slopes and embankments wind their way between palm trees around an immense lake. The 'rough' consists of hard, baked, stony ground. Hard to lose a ball but difficult to play out of, without your ruining your clubs!

In its present state, playing here can best be described as an interesting golfing experience, if passing through the region, en route to other golfing destinations

MARRAKECH

# MARRAKECH

Marrakech the Jewel of the South, is located 240 km south of Casablanca. It is the fourth of Morocco's Imperial Cities and home to just over 1.5 million people, including a growing number of international celebrities, the rich and the famous. An exotic, mystical city, where East meets West, it is the most talked about city in the world - the city of the millennium.

Marrakech is a rail terminus for other parts of Morocco. It also has excellent roads links with the rest of the country and is a good base from which to discover the Atlas Mountains. Marrakech is famous for its fine leatherwork and desert carpets; it is a place where snake charmers, monkey trainers, tooth pullers and fortune-tellers sit beside palaces and monuments of unrivalled refinement. Marrakesh was founded in 1062 and was once the capital of an empire, which stretched from Toledo to Senegal. The city dominates the fertile Haouz Plain at the foot of the snow-capped High Atlas Mountains. This imperial city became an important commercial, cultural and religious crossroad for the entire Maghreb, Andalusia and parts of Black Africa. It has seen the succession of no less than four dynasties, each one leaving behind still visible traces of its identity. The modern city was constructed in 1913 during the French occupation of the country and reflects the European influence.

Throughout history, this city has never failed to leave an indelible mark upon visitors. Sir Winston Churchill was particularly taken by Marrakech and, in his War Memoirs, left this evocative memorial to this intoxicating Moroccan city:

"Here, surrounded by its extensive palm-groves that have sprung out of the desert, the traveller may rest assured that he will never tire of the majestic view of the snow-covered Atlas Mountains. The sun is dazzling and warm, but never unbearably so; the air is sharp and refreshing, yet never unpleasantly cold; the days are perfect, the nights are cool".

"The local inhabitants, dressed in their burnooses of various colours and patterns, are themselves a permanent picture; every countryman is a possible painting, every crowd is a pictorial composition.

"Should anyone be seeking a warm sunny winter, it is to be found in a truly unique setting here in Morocco."

## PLACES OF INTEREST

## JEMAA EL FNA SQUARE

The Jemaa el Fna Square is unique in Morocco. Although a great tourist attraction, tourists make up only a small minority of the crowds, for this is where all of Marrakech converges, to trade, seek advice and to play.

It is a genuine open-air theatre, where you can be enthralled by acrobats, fire-eaters, snake charmers, musicians or storytellers of the "thousand and one night" tales. Simultaneously, you can shop, eat, hire a scribe, and have your hair cut or a tooth pulled.

Shops, souks and cafes surround the square. The best time to visit and soak in the unique atmosphere is after your round of golf, at sunset. Find yourself a place in one of the many rooftop cafes, which overlook the square, order some mint tea and watch the drama unfold before you. The sky turns purple, orange and then deep pink. The atmosphere takes on a smoky nighttime glow from the hundreds of gas lamps that light the sizzling food stalls. Then watch, as if on cue, as the locals arrive to meet, eat and be entertained.

# THE SOUKS

The Souks are North of Jemaa el Fna Square. This area is a vast flourishing labyrinth of narrow streets and alleyways, some covered and some open air. They contain the colourful, highly specialized handicrafts workshops and bazaars for which Marrakech is famous. The easiest point to enter is from the Jemaa el Fna Square.

All manner of necessities and trifles are on sale. Pottery, leather goods, jewellary, wrought iron, clothing, cosmetics and the most bizarre "health foods'. As is the custom, each speciality has its own little neighbourhood.

Leather and cedar wood products are the best buys. Of course, bargaining for a best price is a way of life here.

# KOUTOUBIA MOSQUE

The Koutoubia is visible at 25 km from the city, its stone minaret, (77 metres) is as high as the Notre Dame of Paris. It elegantly defies the peaks of the High Atlas and is a jewel of Islamic architecture. The minaret of the Koutoubia Mosque is one of the three most beautiful minarets of the Almohad era (the others are in Rabat and Seville).

Credit for its completion, towards the end of the 12th Century, goes to Yaqoub el Mansour, the third Almohad sultan.

# EL BAHIA PALACE

Only a century old, the El Bahia Palace was built as a harem residence by Si Ahmed ben Musa, Grand Vizier to Sultan Moulay el Hassan I. It contains richly decorated rooms and exquisite gardens and patios.

## EL BADI PALACE

Little is left of this 16th Century palace, which was once the most beautiful palace in the world and home to Sultan Ahmed El Mansour. The sunken gardens and the vast courtyard remain impressive.

## THE SAADIANS TOMBS

Dating back to the time of the grand Sultan Ahmed El Mansour (1578-1603), these tombs were only discovered in 1917 and, ever since, have not ceased to amaze visitors by their beauty and decorations. They enclose the remains of dignitaries of the Saadian dynasty, considered to this day, to be the protecting saints of the city.

## THE AGDAL AND MENARA GARDENS

Never ending fruit gardens testify to the early genius of agriculture and water distribution techniques. In summer, these terrestrial Gardens of Eden allowed a taste of the pleasures of cascading water, mixed with the whispering leaves on the trees, when the heat elsewhere was unbearable.

## PALMERAIE (PALM GROVE)

Marrakech's famous date palm oasis begins about 7km north of the town on the Casablanca road. Stretching an immense 30,000 acres, the Palmeraie was once a great source of wealth to the reigning Sultans. The area has now become a hideaway of choice for the rich and famous who have built palatial villas within its sandy tracts.

# RECOMMENDED

## PLACES TO STAY

**Palmeraie Golf Palace** – Integrated Golf Hotel and Complex.
5 Star Deluxe Resort.

**Les Jardins de la Palmeraie** BP 1488
Tel (212) (44) 30 10 10 / Fax (212) (44) 30 50 50 or 30 63 66
e-mail : pgp@open.net.ma
web-site : http//www.pgpmarrakech.com

With the 18 hole Golf De La Palmeraie on location, this must surely be the golfers choice and one that is highly recommended by the author. A wonderful, exotic building - typically Moroccan, built using the country's best materials and craftsmen.

It has a wonderful tranquil location a short distance away from the center of Marrakech. Worth a visit even if you are not staying here

All the rooms are luxurious and spacious with all the facilities – satellite, mini-bar, air-conditioning and wonderful views.  The Hotel service is supreme and extremely friendly. A wide range of cuisine in ten elegant restaurants. Four bars to choose from, a nightclub and a shopping mall. What more could a Golfer want?

There are 5 pools and a fully equipped fitness centre if you are still feeling energetic, a Health S pa to relax, if you are not.  Other facilities include beauty salon, tennis courts, ten-pin bowling, pool tables and an equestrian center.

**Hotel Mamounia – Palace De Luxe**
Avenue Bab Jdid
Tel (212) (44) 44 89 81 / Fax (212) (44) 44 49 40 / 44 46 60
e-mail : management@mamounia.com
web site : http//www.mamounia.com
N.B. Golf practice on location.

**Méridien N'Fis – 5***
Avenue de France
Tel (212) (44) 44 87 72 / Fax (212) (44) 44 74 46
N.B. Golf packages available upon request

**Kempinsky Mansour Eddahbi – 5***
Avenue de France
Tel (212) (44) 44 82 22 / Fax (212) (44) 44 90 78

**Kenzi Semiramis – 5 ***
Route de Casablanca – Semlalia
Tel (212) (44) 43 13 77 / Fax (212) (44) 44 71 27 / 44 72 00

## RYADS AND VILLAS

**Les deux Tours**
Rue Ibn Sina BP 513
Tel (212) (44) 32 95 25 /26 / 27
Fax (212)(44) 32 95 23
24 Rooms in 6 luxurious villas in the Palmgrove designed by the famous architect Charles Boccara, inspired by the andalous art of the 14th Century. Clients may rent the whole villas or only the rooms. Food is served upon request.

**Marrakech - Médina**
Fax in Paris 01 43 25 98 77
Fax in Marrakech (212) (44) 39 10 71
Proposes many riads in Marrakech for 2 to 12 persons, with own classification (1 to 4 palm trees)

**Kasbah Agafay**
BP226 40 000 Marrakech Medina
Telephone 212 44 42 09 60/61
Fax 212 44 42 09 70

**Amanjena**
Route de Ouarzazate
Km 12 Marrakech
Tel: 212 4 4403 353
Fax 212 4 4403 477

## Moroccan Cuisine

Moroccan restaurants of most hotels.

**Chez Ali**
Is a must for all visitors to Marrakech.
Good food and a great show.

**La Palmeraie**
Tel : 212 (44) 30 77 30  / (44) 30 93 81
Fax : 212 (44) 30 93 82

**Dar Mounia**
Rue Khalifa
Tel 212 (44) 43 12 41  / 43 66 31

**Dar Yacout**
79 Sidi Ahmed Soussi
Tel (212) (44) 38 29 29

**Dar Marjana**
15 Derb Sidi Ali Taïr
Tel (212) (44) 44 57 34

**Ksar Es saoussan**
3 Derb El Messaoudyenne
Tel (212) (44)  42 60 75

**El Fassia**
222 Ave Mohamed V
Tel  (212) (44) 43 40 60

## Italian Cuisine

**Le Catanzaro**
Rue Tarik Ibn Ziad
Tel (212) (44) 43 37 31

**La Trattoria**
179 Rue Mohamed El Beqal
Tel (212) (44) 43 26 41

## International / French Cuisine

**Bagatelle**
101 Rue de Yougoslavie
Tel (212) (44)  43 02 74

**Chez Jack'Line**
63 Ave Mohamed V
Tel (212) (44) 44 75 47

**Le Jacaranda**
32 Bd Mohamed Zerktouni
(212) (44) 44 72 15

**L'Amandier**
Angle Ave de Paris et Echouhada
Tel (212) (44) 44 72 37

**La Note Gourmande**
Ave de France
Tel (212) (44) 43 85 95

**L'Entrecôte**
55 Bd Mohamed V
Tel (212) (44) 44 94 28

**Villa Rosa**
64 Ave Hassan II
Tel (212) (44) 43 08 32

**Les Cépages**
9 Rue Ibn Zeidoun
Tel (212) (44) 43 94 26

# THE MARRAKECH ROYAL GOLF CLUB

Royal Golf Club of Marrakech

BP 634

Ancienne Route de Ouarzazate

Marrakech

Tel: 212 (44) 40 47 05  / 44 43 41

Fax: 212 (44) 31 08 87

Year opened 1923

18 holes

Par 72

5888 meters

Green fees

Caddies mandatory

Open daily

Marrakech is challenging Rabat as the capital of Moroccan golf. It has three courses, all close to the ancient walled city. The Royal Golf, one of the oldest is a traditional course, deeply rooted in the history of this golfing Kingdom. Churchill, Lloyd George and Eisenhower graced its emerald fairways. It is said that His Majesty the late King Hassan II regarded the course as his favourite. This woodland course is also a favourite with British golfers, as it provides greens that are in top condition, even during winter and a design that is interesting from start to finish.

The course is fairly flat and set against a backdrop of the snow-capped peaks of the Atlas Mountains reaching into an endless blue sky. The Royal is famed for its narrow fairways flanked by a splendid mix of majestic cypress, eucalyptus, olive, palm and orange trees. These provide cooling shade and a mystical and exotic atmosphere. It is such a welcoming course, there can be few lovelier places to play golf.

122

It is not a long course and the smart player determined for a low score, would leave the driver in the bag. The fairways are all fairly straight. Take an extra club for every approach and you will have to play badly not to score well. However, it remains a worthy test of golf and is certainly a long way from your average 'holiday course'. It is difficult to say which is the best hole; the most famous and the signature hole is the 15th a pretty par 3, nicknamed Brigitte Bardot, for reasons which will be obvious when lining up for the tee shot!

The clubhouse is an elegant colonial style building with typical Moroccan detailing and a veranda overlooking the gardens.

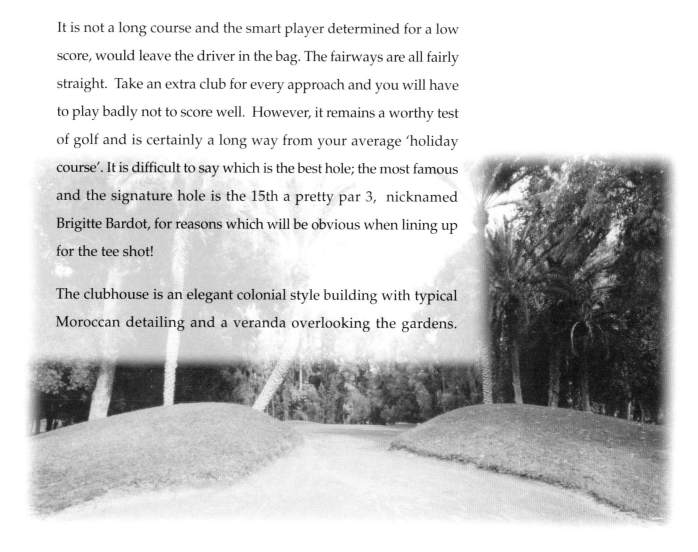

# THE PALMERAIE GOLF PALACE & RESORT

Marrakech

Les Jardins de la Palmeraie

Circuit de la Palmeraie

BP 1488

Marrakech

Tel: 212 (44) 30 10 10

Fax: 212 (44) 30 50 50 / 30 63 66

Year opened 1993

18 holes

Par 72

6214 meters

Green fees

Caddies available

Open daily

The Palmeraie Golf Palace is an outstanding resort with a five star deluxe hotel that is the centerpiece of a golf complex designed by Robert Trent Jones Senior. It is a glorious site and the architect has done it justice, an oasis within an oasis. This acclaimed American genius has created another 18-hole masterpiece, amid an ancient and historic palm grove, with views of the snow-covered peaks of the High Atlas Mountains and where the fairways, greens, golden sand bunkers and lakes are blended together in perfect harmony.

Although designed to take full advantage of the natural features of the landscape, the course is typically American with distinctive bunkering and acres of lakes that come into play on several holes and create a striking contrast with the surrounding desert environment. It forms part of the wonderful residential complex of the Jardins de la Palmeraie; the golf links are not encumbered with an excessive number of buildings, as is very often the case.

On this course, there is not a single straight hole. After the tee shot, the fairways constantly change direction, choosing to wind round a lake, a palm grove or a sand trap. Many of the holes are outstanding. Of the many great holes, the 9th is perhaps the most exciting; it is par 4, dogleg right with water all along one side. One is tempted to reach the group of palm trees on a level with the dogleg at 225 metres from the back tees; should you fail to do so, the penalty is high. The entrance to the flat green is fairly open despite the bunker on the left and the lake on the right. The first nine are pleasant enough; the back nine are quite something!

The course is a challenge, no matter what your handicap and pure joy in terms of the setting and the scenic panorama that unfolds at each hole. The course is largely flat and therefore exposed to the winds, the greens are of a consistently high quality, the rough is kept fairly short to ensure that the golfer can spend more time admiring the view rather than searching for his golf ball. Since its opening, it has hosted several important Championships, both professional and amateur.

In the heart of the links stands the magnificent Moorish styled clubhouse, a short walk away from the hotel, with warm earth colours under a sparkling green tiled roof; a building that reflects the fascinating style of the national architecture. The clubhouse, like the hotel, is sumptuous and offers all the usual amenities.

The Palmeraie Golf Palace Hotel is a genuine five star resort property and a cool oasis of colour, exotic perfumes, fountains and palm trees that will captivate the visitor. Its gourmet restaurants and terraces face the Atlas mountain range. The luxuriously furnished guest rooms all have private bathroom, air-conditioning, satellite TV, telephone, seating area and a small balcony overlooking the gardens, pool area or golf course. For those with boundless energy, there is minigolf, bowling, tennis, squash, horse riding, hammam, sauna, Jacuzzi, massage rooms, gym, nightclub, cycling, billiards and five swimming pools. The complex also boasts substantial conference and banqueting facilities. From the majestic entrance to the most secret nook and cranny, there is an atmosphere of relaxed elegance. Warm friendliness pervades this beautiful hotel in a country already famed for its hospitality.

# AMELKIS GOLF CLUB

Golf D'Amelkis

Km 12

Route de Ouarzazate

Opposite, Golf Royal

Marrakech

Tel: 212 (44) 40 44 14 / 40 30 46

Fax: 212 (44) 43 59 53

Year opened 1995

18 holes

Par 72

6657 meters

Green fees

Caddies available

Open daily

Amelkis Golf Club has rapidly become one of the most frequented in the Kingdom, due not only to the local climate but also to the quality of its facilities. Amelkis, a tough American style course designed by Cabell Robinson, is set in an extraordinary landscape where the beauty of the snow-capped Atlas mountains is contrasted with a Mediterranean panorama of olive and palm trees. The club is part of a modern tourist complex, with individual villas surrounding the course.

Moroccan courses are renowned for their visual appeal, but Amelkis may be the most eye-catching of all and perhaps the most exciting to play. The course was designed with the existing natural surroundings closely in mind; characteristics such as water features have been greatly enhanced during the construction phase and this, together with the planting of several thousand semi-mature trees and the introduction of many new species of flora, has created a variety of habitats and encouraged wildlife to take up home on the site.

It is a huge site, seductively mounded, heavily bunkered and with large greens and expansive, undulating fairways, lakes and fountains. The wide fairways tempt you to open up the shoulders and the greens, although relatively easy to find, will require your most trusted putter to avoid four putting. The approach shots and the putting surface is what Almekis is all about.

The course is well watered and the greens are always in top condition. The most demanding golfers will be challenged by this course's bunkers, rolling terrain, water traps and exotic rough.

The magnificent new clubhouse, possibly the best, certainly the best appointed in all Morocco, is an ochre-coloured traditional style kasbah. It holds sway over the links and creates a tranquil atmosphere ideally suited for relaxing after a game. The catering offered at The Almekis is outstanding, with specialities served either on the terrace or indoors in the elegant, tastefully furnished lounge. The enthusiastic and extremely obliging staff with their green tartan uniform add character and colour, to the whole ambience.

## DRIVING AND CAR HIRE

Drivers must be over 21 and be fully insured against claims by third parties. The insurance is automatic on renting a car. If taking your own vehicle, the European insurance Green Card is required and you will also need the registration document. If your insurance company does not issue Green Card insurance for Morocco (few do), you will need to purchase it in Morocco. Your own national licence is valid, but it does no harm to carry an International Driving Permit as well (it has French and Arabic translations and is available from motoring organisations). An international customs carnet is required for caravans.

The rules of the road are to drive on the right, and give priority to the right. This means that traffic going on to a roundabout has priority over the traffic already engaged. Major roads are well surfaced, minor ones good, with lapses (some treacherous potholes) and mountain roads often not as bad as you may have been led to expect. A toll-funded motorway is gradually being built between Casablanca and Tangier. Tolls are low, at least by European standards. Beware of other drivers.

Fuel is available in towns and along the highway, but fill up before striking out on a long journey away from main roads. An increasing number of petrol stations sell lead-free fuel. Petrol gets cheaper to the south. Parking in towns of any size is likely to cost a few dirhams, collected by an official attendant, who may offer car cleaning services at a price.

The major international hire companies are all represented in Morocco and it is possible to make arrangements to pick up a vehicle at any of the airports. In cities there are always several local companies, who will undercut the rates of the major companies considerably, possibly by as much as half. This will be useful for short rentals (which are proportionately more expensive): but for a rental lasting the whole trip, it may be cheaper to organise a car in advance on a special holiday tariff - either through a travel agent or direct with one of the major companies. Large international companies are likely to have a better network of offices if anything goes wrong with the car.  Car hire prices are usually quoted exclusive of a 19 percent government tax: be sure this has been added to the agreed price.

Cars can also be supplied with a chauffeur, relatively inexpensively, highly recommended for golfing groups leaving the 19th. Chauffeurs normally carry a  mobile phone and therefore tend to drop you off and (look after other clients?) whilst waiting for your call to be picked up. They are on the whole very reliable and an extremely good source of information for restaurants, shopping etc. They tend to stay with you right until you turn in!

# RECOMMENDED CAR RENTAL COMPANIES

## CASABLANCA

**HERTZ**
25 Rue El Oraibi Jilali –
Casablanca
Tel (212) (22) 48 47 10 / Fax
(212) (22) 29 44 03

**BUDGET**
Angle Bd Mohamed V &
Bd de la Résistance N° 55
– Casablanca
Tel (212) (22) 24 86 24 / Fax
(212) (22) 24 86 36
e-mail :
budget@mail.cbi.net.ma

**EUROPCAR**
42 Ave de l'Armée Royale
Tel (212) (22) 31 37 37 / Fax
(212) (22) 31 03 60

**AVIS**
71 Ave de l'Armée Royale
Tel 212 (22) 31 11 38   Fax
(212) 22 31 44 51

## AGADIR

**Avis**
Avenue Hassan II
Tel: 212 (48) 840345

**Budget**
Avenue Mohammed V. Tel:
212 (48) 840762

**Hertz**
Bungalow Marhaba
Avenue Mohammed V
Tel: 212 (48) 840939.

## FEZ

**Avis**
50 Boulevard Chefchaouni.
Tel: 212 (55) 626746

**Budget**
6 Ave Lalla Asmaa
TEL:  212 (55) 620919

**Hertz**
1 Boulevard Lalla Meryern.
Tel: 212 (55) 622812.

## RABAT

**Avis**
7 Rue Abou Faris Marine
TEL:212 (37) 769759

**Budget**
Ave Mohammed V Gare
Once
TEL: 212 (37) 705789

**Europcar**
25 Bis rue Patrice
Lumumba
Tel: 212 (37) 724141

## MARRAKECH

**Avis**
137 Avenue Mohammed V.
Tel:  212 (44) 433727

**Budget**
213 Avenue Mohammed V.
Tel: 212 (44) 431180

**Hertz**
157 Boulevard Mohammed
V.
Tel:  212 (44) 431394

## TANGIER

**Avis**
54 Boulevard Pasteur.
Tel: 212 (39) 933031

**Budget**
7 Avenue du Prince
Moulay Abdellah.
Tel: 212 (39) 948060

**Hertz**
36 Avenue Mohammed V
Tel: 212 (39) 322210

# TRAVEL ESSENTIALS.

## HOW TO GET THERE

## BY AIR

Royal Air Maroc (R.A.M.) the national airline serves London daily out of Heathrow to Casablanca its hub, providing excellent connections on to 14 domestic destinations such as Marrakech, Agadir, Fez and Ouarzazate. There are also 2 non-stop flights to Tangier – RAM has increased its services to a three-time weekly non-stop flight to Marrakech out of Gatwick.
www.royalairmaroc.co.uk

GB Airways, franchise of British Airways to North Africa, also flies to Morocco.
www.britishairways.com

**royal air maroc**

## ROYAL AIR MAROC OFFICES

**Belgium:** 46-48 Place de Broukerie 1000.
Tel: 219 24 50.

**Canada:** 1001 de Maisonneuve Ouest, Suite 440, Montreal. Tel: 285 1619

**France:** 38 Avenue de l'Opera, Paris.
Tel: 44 94 13 30.

**Germany**: Friedenstrasse 9, 60311 Frankfurt 9.
Tel: 236 120/228/229.

**Great Britain:** 205 Regent Street, London W1B
4PE Tel: 0207 439 8854
FAX 020 7287 0127
email: ramlondon@btinternet.com

**Italy:** Via Barbarini 86, Rome.
Tel: (06) 474 58/4744879.

**Netherlands:** Liedstraat 59, 1017 Amsterdam.
Tel: 624 71 88.

**Spain:** Gran Viad de Les Corts Catalnes 636, 6th
Floor, Barcelona. Tel: 301 8474; Calle Princesa 7,
28008, Madrid.
Tel: 547 79 05/06/07.

**Switzerland:** 4 Rue Chantepoulet 2035/1211
Geneva 1.  Tel: 731 5971/5972.

**United States:**  55 East 59th Street, Suite 178,
New York. Tel: (212) 750 5115.

## BY SEA

The most logical point of entry by sea is from Algeciras in southern Spain, across the Strait of Gibraltar to Tangier (around 2 hours) or the Spanish duty-free territory of Ceuta (around 90 minutes). Tangier is better connected to public transport in Morocco. These short hops are the best bet for those in cars, since there are sailings throughout the day. July and August are obviously the busiest period. Passport control takes place on board the boat. You must have your passport stamped before disembarking.

There are also hydrofoil services to Tangier from Algeciras, Gibraltar, and Tarifa (Spain's most southerly town), but these will not run if the sea is too rough; they are also less frequent than the traditional ferries. Spanish car ferries run from Almeria and Malaga to the Spanish duty-free port of Mellilla (6.5 and 7 hours respectively). Finally, there are car ferries run by the Compaigne Marocaine de Navigation from Sète, in southern France, to Tangier or via the Balearic Islands to Nador; the Tangier crossing takes 38 hours.

## ADDRESSES:

**SOUTHERN FERRIES**
179 Piccadilly
London W1V 9DB
Telephone:  0207 491 4968
Fax: 0207 491 3502

**FIRST TRAVEL SERVICES**
76A, Golborne Road
(Off Portobello Road)
London W10    5PS
Tel: 02089697979, Fax:
02089690060
E-mail:
firsttravelservices@yahoo.co.uk

**TOUR AFRICA**
ICC Building
Main Street

Gibraltar

Telephone: 77666

# BY RAIL

Trains leave London Victoria and connect, via the Algeciras ferry, with Tangier, Rabat and Casablanca, by way of Paris (change to Gare d'Austerlitz in Paris).  The total journey time, London to Tangier, is around 48 hours.

# BY ROAD

Two options: you can drive through France to catch the ferry at Sète, or take one of the Algeciras ferries.  Generally, travelling to Morocco by car is expensive (allowing for toll fees in France and Spain as well as ferries, petrol and overnight accommodation). For travel through France, you will need Green Card insurance and for Spain a bail bond, both issued by your regular insurer. Few British insurers are prepared to cover cars in Morocco.  Your best bet is to purchase insurance when you arrive. You will also need to take your Vehicle Registration Document.

## WHAT TO BRING

Although cash tips are common, certain small items are acceptable as gifts, such as ballpoint pens, small notebooks or wrapped sweets, especially for children who have posed for photographs or anyone who has helped you.

## TIME ZONES

Moroccan time is the same as Greenwich Meridian Time.

## CLIMATE

Three types of climate are exhibited in three distinct regions: the coastal regions have warm, dry summers, but are wet for the rest of the year and mild in winter: south of Agadir, the coast is drier where it is free from Atlantic depressions during the winter. Agadir has a well-protected climate, with a narrow range of temperatures: but, in common with the rest of the Atlantic coast, the cold offshore waters can cause cloud and fog. The mountains get hot, dry summers and very harsh winters: parts of the High Atlas are under snow well into the summer. The remainder of the country has a typical continental climate, getting hotter and drier in summer to the south, but temperatures moderated by the sea to the west. In the inland Sahara area, very dry hot summers give way to warm sunny days and cold (sometimes frosty) nights in winter.

## WHAT TO WEAR

Dress for comfort.  Light-coloured lightweight cottons are advisable, and in the south, head protection in the summer sun.  Hotels are rarely dressy, although some four and many five star hotels have formal restaurants where men will feel more comfortable in a jacket and tie and women in a dress.  When touring or sightseeing, let tact be a guide: keep skimpy clothes for the beach and remember that jewellery and smart clothes mark the wealthy tourist visiting a poor country; expensive bags or cameras may also attract more attention than you would like.

## ENTRY REGULATIONS:

## VISAS AND PASSPORTS

Holders of full British passports (but not a British Visitor's passport), and holders of valid United States, Canadian, Irish, Australian, New Zealand or Scandinavian passports need no visa for a stay of up to three months.  Children under 16 without their own passports must have their photograph stamped in the passport of one of their parents.

## CUSTOMS

Clothes, jewellery and personal effects including cameras can be brought into the country temporarily, without formality.  Foodstuffs and medicines, in reasonable quantities for personal use, may also be imported.  Duty-free allowances are 250 grams of tobacco or 200 cigarettes or 50 cigars; one litre of wine, one litre of spirits; a quarter litre of eau de cologne.

Customs procedure on entry will vary according to point of arrival; baggage is often searched and will need to be cleared by a customs official before entering the country.

## HEALTH

No vaccinations are required by the Moroccan government for entry, unless you have come from a recognised infected area (e.g. a yellow fever, cholera or smallpox zone). For your own safety, however, cautious doctors advise inoculations against typhoid, polio, cholera and tetanus. A course of malaria tablets may also be advisable; these are normally taken for a week before, during, and for four to six weeks after travelling. The risk of malaria is highest in the summer; effective insect repellent gels or creams are sensible additional precautions.

Some protection against hepatitis may be useful if travelling in country areas. Injections of immuno-globulin give protection for about four weeks; they are no use for longer trips and potential long-term visitors should consult a medical advisor. Contact with standing fresh water (swimming or paddling in oases, river valleys and lagoons) may carry the risk of bilharzia. Rabies is present: seek medical advice immediately if you are bitten.

Aids: This disease can be transmitted through unprotected sexual contact or medical treatment using infected needles, blood or blood transfusion equipment. Most Moroccan pharmacies now stock disposable needles and clinics and hospitals are usually reliable: check with a consulate or embassy if in doubt over treatment. It is possible to buy medical 'kits' containing sterile hypodermic needles and plasma, which can be carried in case of an emergency.

The most common cause of illness is due to overexposure to the heat or sun, especially when combined with excessive alcohol intake; light cotton clothing, moderate exposure and protective lotions all reduce the risk of sunstroke. Drinking bottled mineral water is recommended, especially when it is very hot.

## ON ARRIVAL

When you arrive you will be given an official form to fill in, stating profession, addresses in Morocco and length of stay. Each time you register at a hotel you are required to fill in a similar form, which is submitted to the police.

## ORIENTATION

Reaching a Moroccan town or city is often a bewildering experience. The largest are divided into the old and new towns. The old town - or medina - is the traditional quarter. Often surrounded by ramparts and entered through grand gateways, it will contain a disorientating maze of narrow streets and souks running between squares. It may also contain the fortified Kasbah - ramparts within ramparts. At the other extreme is the "nouvelle ville" - usually planned and laid out by the French, with grand, straight avenues connecting roundabouts. The grandest avenue is often named after Mohammed V and it is usually here or in the main square of the new town, that you will find the tourist offices. On the roads, there are few problems with navigation; signposts are clear and the long roads have few turnings. It is worth taking local advice about the state of mountain or desert roads at any time of the year, but particularly in the mountains in winter.

## AIRPORT / CITY LINKS

There are taxi services between international airports and their respective towns. With the exception of Casablanca (which, with Rabat, now has a rail link between the airport and the city), distances are small, so, in theory, taxi fares should be low. There are official fare tables published, but you are unlikely to see them around the airport; most of the grand taxis on the airport run are unmetered, and drivers may want to haggle over fares.

There is also a rail service between Casablanca airport and Casablanca and Rabat (departures are in line with flight arrivals) and there is also a bus service between the airports of Agadir and Marrakech and their respective cities.

## ON DEPARTURE

Moroccan money may not be exported. If, on departure, you want to reconvert your dirhams into hard currency, you must show your receipt(s) for the original exchange.

There is no departure tax.

## INTERNAL FLIGHTS

There are internal flights between most cities.

## MONEY MATTERS

The Moroccan dirham (DH) is nominally divided into 100 centimes - but these are sometimes called francs. Recent official rates have hovered around £1 = 16DH and US$1 = 10DH. Check newspapers for the current rates.

There is one simple rule: Moroccan currency may not be imported or exported. Visitors can import as much foreign currency (in cash or travellers' cheques) as they wish: if the value of currency imported is more than 15,000DH, they must fill out a declaration des devices, which should be carried with them throughout the trip.

It is useful, especially if entering Morocco, outside banking hours (e.g. on an evening flight) to have some cash - it will be easier to change at airport exchange kiosks (mostly run by banks), who may refuse travellers' cheques or credit cards.

While in Morocco, travellers' cheques in either pounds or dollars are the safest way of carrying money; though some banks will not handle them, their staff will direct you to those which will do so. Exchange rates are fixed, whether in banks or hotels. Most major banks do not charge commission. At the end of the trip, the total amount of Moroccan currency you have bought can be changed back, but only if exchange receipts are produced. If you run out of money, it is possible to use major credit cards to obtain money in main banks.

## PUBLIC HOLIDAYS

There are two sets of holidays, religious and secular; the one based on the Muslim (lunar) year, and the other on the Western (Gregorian) calendar. For exact dates according to the Western calendar, consult the Tourist Office.

## STATE HOLIDAYS

New Year's Day - 1 January

Manifest of Independence - 11 January

Feast of the Throne – July

Labour Day- 1 May

Youth day - 9 July

Allegiance of Oued Edtahab - 14 August

Green March - 6 November

Independence Day - 18 November

## ELECTRICITY

Most of the country's supply is rated 220 volts, but some places have a 110-volt supply; sockets and plugs are of the continental European type, with two round pins.

## SECURITY AND CRIME

Crime against tourists is not common, but neither is it unknown. Violent attacks or muggings are still less common. What tends to be most intimidating, especially in the imperial cities, is harassment from false guides, who try to force their services on you. The best way to deal with them, if you do not want their help is to decline firmly with good humour. Above all, do not become agitated - it only prompts abuse.

Avoid wearing jewellery, or carrying too much money in the streets: use hotel safe deposit boxes. If you are on the move, prefer a secure pocket or money belt to a shoulder bag for valuables; if you wear a bag, sling the strap over the head, not just the shoulder.

If driving, use similar precautions as at home, do not leave bags visible in the car, always lock your vehicle and leave it empty overnight. Better still, do as the locals do and leave it where an all-night guardian can watch over it (5DH upwards).

If belongings have been stolen, a police report must be made. Do not be put off by hotel staff; insurance companies invariably require a local police report before they will entertain a claim for theft. If tour company representatives are on hand, they may be able to help and should certainly be informed. If your belongings do not arrive at the airport, it is the responsibility of the airline; request a Property Irregularity Form and complete it. Many travel insurance policies will then allow reasonable expenses on clothes and other essentials.

## MEDICAL SERVICES

There are private clinics in all main towns, and government hospitals in many. Consulates may be able to give advice about English-speaking doctors; another avenue is to ask the tour companies' representatives (and notice boards) at hotels. All services will be charged for immediately, except in the cases of need or emergency; if your travel insurance is not explicit on the point of medical treatment, and you have to pay, ask for and keep receipts.

Pharmacies in towns sell many kinds of medicines and contraceptives (but not tampons or sanitary towels - these may be available from general stores in town). Medicines are expensive;

aspirin, insect bite cream and stomach settlers are best bought at home. There is a late night pharmacy in each major town; it is often in the town hall (Municipalité).

## BUSINESS HOURS

Hours vary slightly, but the timetable is based around a two-hour rest in the middle of the day. Standard hours for: Banks: Monday to Friday 8.30 - 11.30 am and 2.30 - 4.30 pm Offices: Monday to Friday 8.30 - noon, 2.30 - 6 pm. Post offices Monday - Saturday 8.30 - 2.00am (at least, the bigger the town, the longer they open). Telephone services, at the same offices, often open in the evenings (the biggest are open 24 hours). Shops: Monday - Saturday 8.30 - noon 2.00 - 6.00 pm. Many shops stay open much later than this; some close on Friday (the Muslim equivalent of the Sabbath) and some are open on Sunday.

## NEWSPAPERS & MAGAZINES

The main newspapers in Morocco are: L'Opinion, Le Matin, Al Alam. The principal business magazine is La Vie Economique.

Enjeux, a current affairs, magazine and Le Matin, and Lamalif is an arts magazine.

English newspapers are available in cities and resort hotels, as are most European papers, the International Herald Tribune and many magazines.

## RADIO & TELEVISION

The television service of Radiodiffusion Télévision Marocain is government-run, along with the associated radio channel. There is also the privately run station funded by subscription. Satellite television is widely available, both in the home and hotels.

A radio station based in Tangier, Radio Méditerranée-Internationale, broadcasts to Algeria, Tunisia, Spain and the South of France. The British World Service from the BBC broadcasts between 6am and midnight (try 16.94m, 17.70MHz). Details of BBC times and wavelengths are available from the British Council in Rabat.

## POST & TELECOMS

Post offices (PTT) deal with postage (if you only need stamps, you can buy these from many tobacconists [tabac]), post restante, telephone and telegraph services.

Since privatisation of the telephone service, it has become increasingly easy to make international calls from phone boxes in the street, arm yourself with plenty of 5DH coins or purchase a telecarte from a nearby tabac (make sure a booth that takes phone cards is at hand). Also increasingly common are private telephone and fax shops, which charge only slightly more than you would pay in a public booth. Calls are also possible from a post office, but you may have to wait. Calls from a hotel are expensive.

## TOURIST OFFICES

### OUTSIDE MOROCCO

Australia: C/o Consulate of Morocco, 11 West Street North, Sydney, NSW 2060.  Tel: 957 6717/922 4999

Belgium:  66 Rue de Marché aux Herbes, 1000 Brussels.  Tel: 512 2182.

Canada:  Place Montreal Trust, 1800 McGill College, Suite 2450, Montreal.  Tel: 48428111.

France:  161 Rue Saint Honoré, Place du Théâtre Français, 0075 Paris.  Tel: 42 60 63 50.

Germany:  Graf Adolf Strasse 59, 4000 Dusseldorf 1. Tel: 911370552.

Great Britain: 205 Regent Street, London W1R 7DE. Tel: 0207 437 0073.

Italy:  Via Larga 23,20122 Milan.  Tel: 58303633.

Spain:  Calle Ventura Rodriguez, 24, 28008 Madrid. Tel: 5427431.

United States:  420 East 46the Street, Suite 1201, New York 10017.  Tel: 5572520/21/22.

### IN MOROCCO

National Tourist Offices (Office National Marocain du Tourisme, ONMT: headquarters in Rabat) are often complemented by a municipal Syndicat d'initiative. Both can give plans, maps, and advice and provide guides, but the ONMT are usually better staffed, with more guides on hand.  Most offices are open Monday to Saturday mornings from 8am.

Agadir:  Place Heritier Sidi Mohammed (off street: on first floor level of paved square opposite post office). Tel: (08) 840207.

Casablanca:  55 Rue Omar Slaoui.  Tel: (02) 2711177.

Fes:  Place de la Résistance, Boulevard Moulay Youseef.  Tel: (05) 623460/626279.

Marrakech: Place Abd el Moumen Ben Ali, Boulevard Mohammed V.  Tel: (04) 436239.

Meknes:  Place Administrative.  Tel: (05) 524426.

Ouarzazate:  Avenue Mohammed V.  Tel: (04) 882485.

Oujda:  Place du 16 Août.  Tel: (06) 685361.

Rabat:  22 Avenue al Jazair (Ave d'Algier).  Tel: (07) 730562.

Tangier:  29 Boulevard Pasteur.  Tel: (09) 948661.

Tetouan:  30 Avenue Mohammed V.  Tel: (09) 961915.

## EMBASSIES & CONSULATES

Canada:  13 Bis Rue Jaffar al-Sadak, Agdal, Rabat.  Tel: (07) 772880.

France:  3 Rue Sahourin (Agdal).  Tel: (07) 777822.

Germany:  7 Zankat Mednine, Rabat.  Tel: (07) 769692.

Great Britain:  17 Boulevard de la Tour Hassan, Rabat.  Tel: (07) 720905/06.  There is also a consul in Tangier.  Tel:  (09) 941557.

Italy:  2 Rue Idriss el Azhar, Rabat.  Tel: (07) 766598.

Netherlands:  40 Rue de Tunis, Rabat.  Tel (07) 73512/3.

Spain:  13 Zankat Mednine, Rabat.  Tel: (07) 708989/707980.2

USA:  2 Avenue de Marrakech, Rabat.  Tel: (07) 762265.

# RECOMMENDED TRAVEL COMPANIES

## IN MOROCCO:

For Information and Literature
Call the **Moroccan National Tourist Office**
205, Regent Street W1B  4HB

Tel : 0207 -437 0073
Fax : 0207 -734 8172
Email : mnto@btconnect.com
Web : www.tourism-in-morocco.com

## IN ENGLAND (in alphabetical order) :

**AARDVARK SAFARIS LIMITED**
RBL House
Ordnance Road
Tidworth
Hants SP9 7QD
Tel: 01980-849160 Fax: 01980-849161
Email: mail@aardvarksafaris.com

www.aardvarksafaris.com

**ABERCROMBIE AND KENT**
Sloane Square House.
Holbein Place.
London SWI W 8NS
Tel:0845 50700610 Fax: 0845 0700 607
Email: info@abercrombiekent.co.uk
www.abercrombiekent.com

**ACACIA EXPEDITIONS LTD**
Lower Ground Floor, 23A Craven Terrace
Lancaster Gate. London W2 3QH
Tel: 0207 - 706 4700 Fax: 0207 - 706 4686
Email: acacia@afrika.demon.co.uk

www.acacia-africa.com

**AIRTOURS HOLIDAYS**
Holiday House
Sandrok Park, Sandbrook Way
Rochdale OL11  1SA
Tel:0870 608 1955 (reservations )
Tel:01706 74 2000
Fax: 01706 742 650
www.airtours.co.uk

**ALECOSS TRAVEL LTD**
(Fully bonded Tour Operator, ATOL 5396)
5, Baker Street
London W1U  8ED
Tel: 020 7224 4652   Fax : 020 7935 9313
Email: sales@alecoss.co.uk
www.alecoss.co.uk
www.morocco4golf.com

**AMOUN TRAVEL & TOURS**
56 Kendal Street
London W2 2BP
Tel: 0207 - 402 3100 Fax: 0207 - 402 3424
Email: sales@aniountravel.co.uk
www.amountravels.co.uk

**ARCHERS DIRECT**
3rd Floor Wren Court
17 London Road Bromley
Kent BRI IDE
Reservations : 0870-751 2000 Fax: 0208 - 313 1670
Admin: 0870-750 0999
Email: mail@archersdirect.co.uk
www.archersdirect.co.uk

**BALES WORLDWIDE**
Bales House , Junction Road, Dorking, Surrey RH4 3HL
Tel: 0870241 3208/0870241 3212 Fax: 013067 40048
Email: enquiries@balesworldwide.com
www.balesworldwide.com

**BEST OF MOROCCO**
Seend Park. Seend
Wiltshire SN12 6NZ
Tel: 01380 - 828 533 Fax: 01380 - 828 630
Email: morocco@morocco-travel.com
www.morocco-travel.com

**BRIDGE**
Bridge House,
55-59 High Road,
Broxbourne, Herts EN10 7DT
Tel: 0870 191 7185 Fax:01992 45 6609
cities@bridge-travel.co.uk

**BRITISH AIRWAYS HOLIDAYS**
The Beehave,Gatwick Airport
West Sussex RH 6 OLA
Tel: 01293 664 239 Fax: 01293-664 218
www.baholidays.co.uk

**CADOGAN HOLIDAYS**
Cadogan House, 9-10 Portland Street
Southampton, Hampshire SO 14 7EB
Tel: 023 8082 8304 Fax: 02380 228601
Reservations: 023-80828304
www.cadoganholidays.com

**CARTE BLANCHE INTERNATIONAL**
27 Albert Square
London SW8 IDA
Tel: 0207 - 735 9923 Fax: 0207 - 735 7633
Email: carteblanche@mail.com
www.villasandyachts.com

**CLUB MED**
Kennedy House
1 15 Hammersmith Road
London W 14 OQH
Tel: 0207- 348 3333 ( or 0700 Club Med

reservations)
Fax: 0207 - 348 3336
Email: admin.uk@clubrned.corn
www.cilibmed.com

**CONDOR TRAVEL (UK) LTD**
234 Earls Court Road, London SW5 9AA
Tel: 0207 - 373 0495 Fax: 0207 - 835 1052

**CONTIKI HOLIDAYS**
Wells House
15 Elmfield Road
Bromley
Kent  BR1   1LS
Tel: 0208290 6777  Fax; 02082254223
E-mail: travel@contiki.co.uk
www.contiki.com

**COX & KINGS**
Gordon House
10 Greencoat Place
London SWIP IPH
Tel: 0207 - 873 5000 Fax: 0207 - 630 6038
Email: Cox.Kings@coxandkings.co.uk

**CRESTA HOLIDAYS**
Tabley Court
Victoria Street
Altrincham Cheshire WA 14 IEZ
Tel: 0870 - 161 0900 Fax: 0870 -169 0797

**CRYSTAL HOLIDAYS**
King's Place. Wood Street
Kingston-lipon-Thames, Surrey KTI IJY
Tel: 0870 - 848 7015 Fax: 0208 -939 0417
Email: travel@crystalholidays.co.uk
www.crystalholidays.co.uk

**CV TRAVEL**
43 Cadogan Street, Chelsea
London SW3 2PR
Tel: 0207 - 591 2810 Fax: 0207 - 591 2802
24 hr brochure service : 0870 - 603 9018
Email: cv.travel@dial.pipex.com

**DANCE HOLIDAYS**
108 New Bond Street
London WIY 9AA
Tel: 0207 499 5232 Fax: 0207 499 5233
Email: enquiries@danceholidays.com
www.danceholidays.com

**DESTINATION GOLF**
26 Crown Road, St Margarets
Twickenham TWI 3EE
Tel: 0208 - 891 5151 Fax: 0208 - 891 2455
Email: info@destinationgolf.co.uk
www.destinationgolf.co.uk

**DISCOVER LTD**
Timbers, Oxted Road
Godstone, Surrey RH9 8AD
Tel:  01883 - 744 392 Fax: 01883 - 744 913
Email:info@discover.ltd.uk
www.kasbahdutoubkal.com

**DISCOVER ADVENTURE**
4 Netherhampton Cottage,
Netherhampton Road
Netherhampton Salisbury, Wiltshire
SP2  8PX
Tel: 01722741123
Fax: 01722741150
e-mail: info@discoveradventure.com
www.discoveradventure.com

**DRAGOMAN & ENCOUNTER**
2000 Camp Green, Debenham,
Stowmarket
Suffolk IP14  6LA
Tel: 01728 - 861 133/ 862311 Fax: 01728 - 861 127
Email: info@dragoman.co.uk
www.dragoman.co.uk ,
www.encounter.co.uk

**DRIVELINE**
Greenleaf House
Darkes Lane Potters Bar
EN6  1AE
Tel: 0870757 7575  Fax: 01707649 126
enquiries@driveline.co.uk

**ELEGANT RESORTS LTD**
The Old Palace
Chester CH I IRB
Tel: 0870 - 3333 370 Fax: 0870 - 3333 371
Email: cnquiries@elegantresorts.co.uk
www.elegantresorts.co.uk

**EQUITOUR**
15 Grangers Place, Bridge Street
Witney,Oxford OX28  4BS
Tel: 01993 849 489 Fax: 01993849747
Email: llequitour@aol.com
www.equitour.com

**EXLUS1VE GOLF TOURS**
PO Box 201 I
Thrnton heath CR7 8ZE
Tel: 0208-679 65 71 Fax: 0208 679 0671
Email: sales @exclusivegolf.co.uk
www.exclusivegolf.co.uk

**EXODUS TRAVELS**
9 Weir Road
London SW12 OLT
Tel: 0208 - 675 5550 Fax: 0208 - 673 0779
24hr brochure / tact sheets: 0208 - 673 0859
Email: sales@exodustravels.co.uk
www.exodlis.co.uk

**EXPLORE WORLDWIDE LTD**
I Frederick Street. Aldershot
Hants GUI I ILQ
Tel: 01252-760 000 Fax: 01252-760 001
Brochure Request: 01252-760100
Email: info@exploreworldwide.com
www.exploreworldwide.com

**FAR FRONTIERS LTD**
The Pound Ampney Crucis
Gloucestershire GL7 5SA
Tel: 01285 850 926 Fax: 01285 851 575
Email: info@farfrontiers.com
www.farfrontiers.com

**FIRST TRAVEL SERVICES**
76A, Golborne Road
(Off Portobello Road)
London W10 5PS
Tel: 0208 969 79 79 Fax: 0208 969 0060
E-mail: firsttravelservices@yahoo.co.uk

**FLEETWAY TRAVEL**
6th Floor 388-392
Oxford Street London W1C IJU
Tel: 0207 - 870 9700 Fax: 0207 -870 9770
www.fleetway.com

**GANE & MARSHALL
INTERNATIONAL**
98 Crescent Road
New Barnet
Herts, EN4 9RJ
Tel: 0208 - 441 9592 Fax: 0208 - 441 7376
Email:
holidays@ganeandmarshall.co.uk
www.ganeandmarshall.co.uk

**GOLDENJOY HOLIDAYS**
36 Mill Lane
London NW6 ITQ
Tel: 0207-794- 9818 Fax: 0207-794 9850
Email: ellen@goldenjoy.co.uk

**GREATDAYS TRAVEL GROUP**
Travel House 2 Stamford Park Road
Altrincham, Cheshire WA15 9EN
Tel: 0161 928 9333 Fax: 0161 928 0078
Email: incentive@greatdays.co.uk
www.greatdays.co.uk

**GREENSLADES TRAVEL**
2nd Floor, 51-52 High Street
Taunton, Somerset TAI 3PR
Tel: 01823 -330 217 Fax: 01823 336883
Email: enquiries@greenslades.co.uk
www.greenslades.co.uk

**GUERBA WORLD TRAVEL LTD**
Wessex House ,40 Station Road,
Westbury
Wilshire BA13 3NJ
Tel: 01373 826611 Fax:0137385835)
Email: info@guerba.co.uk
www.guerba.co.Uk

**H-C TRAVEL**
16 High Street, Overton
Hampshire RG25 3HA
Tel: 01256-770 775 Fax: 01256-771 773
Email: david@hctravel.com
www.hctravel.com

**HF HOLIDAYS**
Imperial House, Edgware Road
London NW9 5AL

Tel: 0208-905 9556 Fax: 0208 205 0506
Email: info@hfholidays.co.uk

**HEADWATER HOLIDAYS**
The Old School House
Chester Road, Castle
Northwich Cheshire CW8 1LE
Tel: 01606 720033 Fax: 01606 6720034
Email: info@headwater.com
www.headwater-holidays.co.uk

**HAYES AND JARVIS**
Hayes House, 152 King Street
London W6 OQU
Tel: 0870 - 898 9890 Fax: 0208-741 0299
Brochure Requests: 0870 - 892 8280
Email: Res@Hayes-Jarvis.com

**INSIGHT HOLIDAYS**
Gareloch House, 6 Gareloch Road
Port Glasgow PA14 5XH
Tel: 0870 51-43-433 Fax: 01475-742 073
Email:
reservations@insightvacations.co.uk

**INTERNATIONAL CHAPTERS**
47-51 St.Jotins Wood High Street
London NW8 7NJ
Tel: 020 - 7722 0722 Fax: 020 - 7722 9140
Email: info@villa-rentals.com
www.villa-rentals.com

**INTERNATIONAL TRAVEL
CONNECTIONS**
Concorde House
Canal Street
Chester CH1 4EJ
Tel: 0870 751 9340 Fax: 0870 751 9419
E-mail: cc@itc-uk.com
www.itcclassics.co.uk

**JAGGED GLOBE**
Fondor Studios
45 Moweray Street, Shefield S3 8EN
Tel:0114276 3322 Fax:0114276 3344
E-mail: expeditions@jagged-globe.co.uk
www.jagged-globe.co.uk

**KE ADVENTURE TRAVEL**
32 Lake Road, Keswick
Cumbria CA12 5DQ
Tel: 017687 739 66 Fax; 017687 74693
E-mail:keadventure@enterprise.net
www.keadventure.com

**KUONI TRAVEL**
Kuoni House, Dorking
Surrey RH5 4AZ
Tel: 01306 740 888
Fax: 01306744 487
worldclass@kuoni.co.uk
www.kuoni.co.uk

**LIBRA HOLIDAYS**
7B, High Street
Herts EN5 5UE
Tel: 0870 241 5127
Fax: 0208 275 5515

E-mail: priceright@libraholidays.net

**LEGER HOLIDAYS**
Sunway House
Canklow Meadows, Rotherdam
S60 2XR
Tel: 01709 839 839 / 01709 830 333
E-mail: reservations@leger.co.uk
www.leger.co.uk

**NOMADIC EXPEDITIONS**
22B Barkham Ride,Finchampstead
Berkshire RG40 4EU
Tel: 0870-2201718 Fax: 0870 220 17 19
Email: info@nomadic.co.uk
www.nomadic.co.uk

**MARRAKESH EXPRESS**
97-99 Pread Street, Paddington,
London,W2 I NT
Tel: 020 7402 3220 (Sales) 020 7402 3229
(Admin)
Tel: 0808100 2774 Fax: 020 74 02 3241
Email: info@marrakesh-express.co.uk
www.marrakesh.express.co.uk

**MARTIN RANDALL TRAVEL LTD**
10 Barley Mow Passage, Chiswick
London W4 4PH
Tel: 0208-742 3355 Fax: 0208-742 7766
Email: info@martinrandall.co.uk
www.martintrandall.com

**MEDITERRANEAN EXPERIENCE
LTD**
767 High Road
London N12 8LH
Tel: 0208 445 6000
Fax:0208 445 7111
E-mail: sales@themed.net
www.themed.net

**MOROCCO MADE TO MEASURE**
I st Floor, 69 Knightsbridge
London SWIX 7RA
Tel: 0207-235 0123/2110 Fax: 0207-235
3851
Email: clmltd@aol.com

**MOROCCO REDISCOVER**
92A, Church Street
Tewkesbury Glos GL20 5RS
TEL: 08707 406 306
Fax : 08707 406 316
E-mail: morocco@rediscover .co.uk
www.rediscover.co.uk

**MOTION TOURS & TRAVEL**
1-2 Hanover Street
London W1R 9WB
Tel: 0207 629 9777 Fax; 0207 629 9333
Email; motion@btinternet.com
www.motion-europe.com

**NATURALLY MOROCCO**
Flill House, Llansteffan
Camarthen SA33 5JG - WALES
Tel: 01267-241999

Email: info@moroccoecotours.com
www.moroccoecotolirs.com

**NOMADIC EXPEDITIONS**
22B Barkham Ride Finchampstead
Berkshire RG40 4 EU
Tel: 0870 220 17 18 Fax: 0870 220 17 19
Email: info@nomadic.co.uk

**NOMADIC THOUGHTS**
81Brondesbury Road
London NW6 6BB
Tel: 0207-604 4408 Fax: 0207-604 4407
uknomadic@aol.com

**OASIS TOURS**
37 Market Place
Kingston Upon Thames
Surrey KT I IJQ
Tel: 0208-296 8877 Fax: 0208-296 991 I
email: info@oasistours.co.iik
www.oasistours.co.uk

**PANORAMA HOLIDAYS**
Panorama House
Vale Road
Portslade Sussex BN41 IHP

Tel: 0870 7595595 Fax : 01273-427 111

Panorama@pavilion.co.uk

**PANWORLD HOLIDAYS**
Greekorama House, 8 Great Chapel
Street
London W1V 3AG
Tel : 0207-734 2562
Fax: 0207-287 0554

**PRESTIGE HOLIDAYS**
1 Fridays Court, High Street
Ringwood, Hants BH24 1JA
Tel: 01425-480 400 Fax: 01425-470 139

**PROSPECT MUSIC & ARTS TOURS**
36 Manchester Street
London W1U 7LH
Tel: 0207-486 5705 Fax : 0207-486 5868
Email: sales@prospecttours.com

**RAMBLERS HOLIDAYS**
Box 43, 2 Church Road, Welvwyn
Garden City Hertfordshire AL8 6PQ
Tel: 01707-331 133 Fax: 01707-333 276
Email: info@ramblersholidays.co.uk
www.ramblersholidays.co.uk

**SHERPA EXPEDITIONS**
131A Heston Road, Hounslow
Middlesex TW5 0RF
Tel: 0208-577 2717 Fax: 0208-572 9788
Email: sales@sherpaexpeditions.com
www.sherpaexpeditions.com

**SIMPLY TRAVEL**
Kings House, Wood Street
Kingston-upon-Thames Surrey KT1

1SG
Tel: 0208 - 541 2212 Fax: 0208 - 541 2282
Email: winter.sun@simply-travel.com
www.simply-travel.com

**SOLO'S HOLIDAYS**
54-58 Hight Street
Edgware, Middlesex HA8 7EJ
Tel: 0208 9512800 Fax: 0208 951 1051
E-mail: travel@solosholidays.co.uk
www.solosholidays.co.uk

**SOVEREIGN CITIES AND SHORT BREAKS**
First Choice House, London Road
Crawley West Sussex RH10 2GX
Tel : 08705 - 768 373
Fax: 01293 457 742

**STEPPES EAST**
51 Castle Street
Cirencester, Gloucestershire GL7 1QD
Tel: 01285-651010 Fax: 01285-885888
Email: sales@steppeseast.co.uk

**SUNWAY HOLIDAYS LTD**
The Sunway Travel Group
114 Lower Georges Street
Dun Laoghaire
Co. Dublin, Ireland
Tel: 00-353-1-2886828 Fax: 00-353-1-2885187
Email: claire@sunway.ie
www.sunway.ie

**SUNWAY HOLIDAYS**
The Sunway Travel Group
P.O. Box 1680
Slough PDO SL1 7XX
Tel: 01628 - 660 001 Fax: 01628 - 602 859

**SUNWORLDWIDE HOLIDAYS**
35B, Bellgrove Road, Welling, Kent
DA16 3PR
Tel: 0208 3011220 Fax: 0208 301 1256
E-mail: info@
sunworldwideholidays.co.uk
www.sunworldwideholidays.co.uk

**TARIK TRAVEL**
9 Windy Hall, Fishguard Pembs SA65 9DP
Tel: 01348 874 361
Fax: 01348 874 380
Email: xfr30@dial.pipex.com

**THE IMAGINATIVE TRAVELLER**
14 Barley Mow Passage
Chiswick London W4 4PH
Tel: 0208-742 8612 Fax: 0208-742 3045
Brochure Request: 0800316 1404
Email: info@imaginative-traveller.com
Www.imaginative-traveller.com

**THE MEDITERRANEAN EXPERIENCE**
767 High Road
London N12 8LH
Tel: 0208 445 6000 Fax: 0208 445 7111
e-mail: sales@themed.net

www.themed.net

**THOMSON BREAKAWAY**
Centenary House
3 Water Lane, Richmond
Surrey TW9 1TJ
Tel: 08706061476 Fax: 0208-210 4269

**TIM BEST TRAVEL**
68 Old Brompton Road
London SW7 3LQ
Tel: 0207 591 0300 Fax: 0207 591 0301
tbest@timbesttravel.com
www.timbesttravel.com

**TIME OFF Ltd**
1 Elmfield Park, Bromley, Kent
BR1 1LU
Tel: 0870 584 6363 /0845 733 66 22
Email: info@timeoff.co.uk
www.timeoff.co.uk

**TRAILMASTERS INTERNATIONAL**
P.O. Box 4 Llanfyllin, Powys
SY22 5 WA
Tel: 01691649194 Fax: 01691648500
E-mail: trailmasters@compuserve.com

**TRAFALGAR TOURS**
15 Grosvenor Place
London SW1X 7HH
Tel: 0207 2357090 Fax: 0207 873 8614
www.trafalgartours.com

**TOP DECK TRAVEL**
125 Earl's Court Road
London SW5 9RH
Tel: 0207-370 4555
Fax: 0207 835 1820
E-mail: res@topdecktravel.co.uk
www.topdecktravel.co.uk

**TRAILFINDERS**
194 kensington high street
London W8 7RG
Tel: 0207 938 3939 Fax: 0207 937 9294
www.trailfinders.com

**TRAVELBAG ADVENTURES**
15 Turk Street, Alton
Hants GU34 1AG
Tel: 01420-541 007 Fax: 01420-541 022
Email: sales@travelbag-adventures.com
Www.travelbag-adventures.com

**TRAVEL PATH**
P.O. Box 32, Grantham
Lincs NG31 7JA
Tel: 01476-570 187 Fax: 01476-572 718
Email: colin@travelpath-uk.com

**TRAVELSCENE**
11-15 St.Anns Road
Harrow Middlesex HA1 1LQ
Tel: 0208-427 8800 Fax: 0208 -861 5083
E-mail: reservations@travelscene.co.uk
www.travelscene.co.uk

**TRIBES**

12 The Business Centre
Earl Soham, Woodbridge
Suffolk IP13 7SA
Tel: 01728-685 971 Fax: 01728-685 973
Email: info@tribes.co.uk
www.tribes.co.uk

**VOYAGES JULES VERNE**
21 Dorset Square-
London NW1 6QG
Tel: 0207-616 1000 Fax: 0207-723 8629
Email: sales@vjv.co.uk
www.vjv.co.uk

**WALKS WORLDWIDE**
15 Main Street
High Bentham LA2 7LG
Tel: 015242 622 55
Fax:015242 62229
Email: info@walksworldwide.com
www.walksworldwide.com

**WESTERN & ORIENTAL TRAVEL**
King House 11 Westbourne Grove
London W2 4UA
Tel: 0207 313 6600Fax: 0207313 6601
E-mail: info@westernoriental.com
www.westernoriental.com

**WILDCAT BIKE TOURS LTD**
Stirling Enterprise Park
Unit 111 John Player Building
Stirling FK7 7RP
Tel/Fax: 01786 464333/ 07802 470880
Email: enq@wildcat-bike-tours.co.uk
Www.wildcat-bike-tours.co.uk

**WORLDWIDE ADVENTURES ABROAD**
Unit H/04 Staniforth Estates
Main Street, Hackenthorpe
Sheffield, Yorks S12 4LB
Tel : 0114-247 3400 Fax: 0114-251 3210
Email: info@adventures-abroad.co.uk
www.adventures-abroad.com

**WORLD EXPEDITIONS**
3, Northfields Prospect
Putney Bridge Road
London SE 1PE
TEL: 0208 870 2600 FAX: 0208870 2615
Email:
enquiries@worldexpeditions.co.uk
www.worldexpeditions.co.uk

**WATER BY NATURE RAFTING JOURNEYS**
Wessex House, 127 High Street
Hungerford, Berkshire RG17 0DL
Tel: 01488680825 Fax: 01488685055
Email: rivers@waterbynature.com
www.waterdbynature.com

# MAJOR HOTEL CHAINS WITH PROPERTIES IN MOROCCO

**ACCOR HOTELS INTERNATIONAL**
255 Hammersmith Road

London W6 8 SJ
Tel: 0845 601 4768
Fax: 020 8283 4650
www.accorhotel.com

Agadir : Mercure Les Almohades / Ibis Moussafir , Coralia Club La Kasbah
El Jadida : Sofitel Royal Golf El Jadida
Casablanca : Mercure les Almohades /Ibis Moussafir
Fez : Ibis Moussafir / Sofitel Palais Jamai
Marrakech : Ibis Moussafir , Sofitel Marrakech, Coralia Club Palmariva,
Oujda : Ibis Moussafir
Rabat :Ibis Moussafir /Sofitel Diwan/Mercure shehrazade
Tangier : Mercure Les Almohades, Ibis Moussafir
Essaouira : Sofitel Thalassa Mogador
Tetouan : Sofitel Thalassa Marina Smir
Meknes : Sofitel Marina Smir

**AMAN RESORTS**:

Pegasus Solution
14th Floor-Quadrant House, the Quadrant
Sutton, Surrey SM2 5AR
Tel: 0800 251840
Email: info @amanresorts.corn

**MARRAKESH**: Amanjena

**BASS HOTELS & RESORTS**
Heathrow Boulevard, Building 4
280 Bath Road, West Drayton UB7 ODQ
Tel: 0800-897 121 Fax: 0108-754 7551
Email: hi-hotelreservations@basshotels.com
www.basshotels.com

**CASABLANCA :** Crowne Plaza

**CLUB MED**
Kennedy House
115 Hammersmith Road
London W14 OQH
Tel: 0207 348 3333 Fax: 0207 348 3335
www.clubmed.co.uk

Clubs in: Agadir/ Marrakech/ Ouarzazate/Restinga/Al Hoceima/Tangier/Smir.

**CAPITAL HOTEL RESERVATIONS**
32 Bath Road, Chiswick
London, W4 ILW
Tel: 0208-742 3760 Fax: 0208-944 9298
Email: reservations@capitalhotels.com
www.capitalhotels.com

Casablanca : Hyatt Regency / Sheraton / Safir / Holiday Inn Crowne Plaza/Idou Anfa/Royal Mansour
Fez : Jnan Palace /

151

www.lemeridien-hotels.com

**Casablanca :** Le Royal Mansour Meridien
**Fez** : Les Merinides Meridien
**Ouarzazate :** Le Berbere Palace Meridien
**Rabat** : La Tour Hassan Meridien
**Marrakech :** Le Meridien N'fis

## RELAIS DU GOLF
Delegate House
The Springs , North Stoke
Wallingperd, Oxon 0X106 BE
Tel: 0149F833633 Fax: 01491 833488
www.relaisdugolf.com

## MARRAKESH
**Palmeraie Golf  Palace & Resort**

## SOL MELIA
3rd Floor, Room 56
The Fruit & Wool Exchange
Brushfield Street, Londonbl 6EP
Tel: 0800-962 720 Fax: 0800-895 444
www.solmelia.es

Agadir Melia Al Madina Salam
Casablanca Melia Riad Salam
Marrakech: Melia Tichka Salam
Taroudant Melia Palais Salam

## SPECIAL HOTELS
Silver House 31-35 Break Street
London WIR3LD
Tel: 020-74403859 Fax: 020-7437 0991
Reservations: 0870 606 1296
Email: info® special hotels.com
www.specialhotels.com

## MARRAKESH
**La Mamounia**

## STARWOOD HOTELS & RESORTS
C/O Parklane Sheraton Hotel
Piccadilly, London WIY 8BX
Tel: 0800-353535 Fax: 0207-499 1965
www.sheraton.com

Agadir: Sheraton
Casablanca: Sheraton
Fez: Sheraton
Marrakech: Sheraton

## THE LEADING HOTELS OF THE WORLD
Avenfield House
118-127 Park Lane
London WIK7LH
Tel: 0800-181 123 Fax: 0207-493 0755
Email: info@lhw.com
www.lhw.com

Marrakech : La Marnounia
Casablanca : Le Royal Mansour Meridien

## VIRGIN HOTEL COLLECTION
120CampdenHillRoad
London W8 7AR
Tel: 0800-716 919 Fax: 01642-701 874
Email:
hotel.reservations@virgin.co.uk
www.virgin.com

Marrakech : Kasbah Tamadot